Air Fryer Cookbook for Beginners

1200-Day of Simple, Affordable, and Tasty Recipes to Help you Keep Healthly and Lose Weight. Includes 4 Weeks Meal Plan

Sarah Green

Table of Contents

What Is Air Frying?..5
Air Fryer Benefits 5
Is an Air Fryer Useful? 5
Air Fryer- Healthier 5
Features 6
Tips On Cleaning An Air Fryer: 6
Air Fryer Breakfast Recipes 8
1. EASY HARD BOILED EGGS 8
2. EASY CHERRY TURNOVERS 8
3. TASTY BAKED EGGS 9
4. BREAKFAST EGG BOWLS 9
5. BLUEBERRY MUFFINS 9
6. LOADED HASH BROWNS 10
7. AIR FRYER SAUSAGE BREAKFAST CASSEROLE 11
8. AIR FRYER BAKED EGG CUPS W/ SPINACH & CHEESE .. 11
9. AIRFRYER FRENCH TOAST STICKS RECIPE 12
10. AIR FRYER BREAKFAST FRITTATA 12
11. BREAKFAST POTATOES IN THE AIR FRYER ... 13
Air Fryer Side Dishes & Dinner Recipes.................... 13
12. 3 INGREDIENT FRIED CATFISH 13
13. BANG BANG FRIED SHRIMP 14
14. FRIED SHRIMP SANDWICH RECIPE 14
15. EASY ROASTED WHOLE CHICKEN 15
16. BEEF TACO FRIED EGG ROLLS 16
17. PARMESAN TRUFFLE OIL FRIES 17
18. LOW-FAT WEIGHT WATCHERS MOZZARELLA CHEESE STICKS 17
19. CARROTS (THREE WAYS) 18
20. BUTTERNUT SQUASH (HOME FRIES) 19
Air Fryer Main & Lunch Recipes 19
21. SEXY AIR-FRIED MEATLOAF 19
22. HAM AND MOZZARELLA EGGPLANT BOATS 20
23. LEFTOVER TURKEY AND MUSHROOM SANDWICH .. 20
24. ITALIAN SAUSAGE PATTIES 21
25. AIR-FRIED POPCORN CHICKEN GIZZARDS 21
26. AIR FRYER CRAB RANGOON 22
27. AIR FRYER CAULIFLOWER FRIED RICE 22
28. AIR FRYER WIENER SCHNITZEL 23
29. AIR FRYER STEAK AND CHEESE MELTS 23
30. AIR FRYER SALMON FOR ONE 24
31. EASY AIR FRYER FRENCH TOAST STICKS 24
32. AIR FRYER FISH STICKS 25
33. AIR FRYER KETO CHICKEN WINGS 25
34. AIR-FRIED MEATLOAF 26
35. AIR-FRIED CRUMBED FISH 26
36. AIR FRYER RANCH PORK CHOPS 27
37. AIR FRYER RIB-EYE STEAK 27
38. AIR-FRIED SESAME-CRUSTED COD WITH SNAP PEAS 28
39. AIR FRYER MEATBALLS 28
40. AIR FRYER HOT DOGS 29
41. AIR FRYER BAKED POTATOES 29
42. CRUMBED CHICKEN TENDERLOINS (AIR FRIED) 30
43. AIR FRYER POTSTICKERS 30
44. HAM AND MOZZARELLA EGGPLANT BOATS 31
45. LEFTOVER TURKEY AND MUSHROOM SANDWICH .. 31
46. ITALIAN SAUSAGE PATTIES 32
47. AIR-FRIED POPCORN CHICKEN GIZZARDS 32
48. AIR FRYER CRAB RANGOON 33
49. MEXICAN-STYLE AIR FRYER STUFFED CHICKEN BREASTS 33
50. AIR FRYER CHIMICHANGAS 34
51. BREADED AIR FRYER PORK CHOPS 35
52. AIR FRYER CRAB RANGOON 35
53. LEMON-GARLIC AIR FRYER SALMON 36
54. AIR-FRIED CRUMBED FISH 36
55. LUNCH EGG ROLLS 37
56. VEGGIE TOAST 37
57. AIR FRYER RANCH PORK CHOPS 37

#	Title	Page
58.	FROZEN CHICKEN WINGS (NO THAW)	38
59.	RIB-EYE STEAK	38
60.	AIR-FRIED SESAME-CRUSTED COD WITH SNAP PEAS	39

Air Fryer Seafoods Recipes 39

#	Title	Page
61.	AIR FRYER COCONUT SHRIMP	39
62.	PECAN CRUSTED SALMON	40
63.	BROILED TILAPIA DONE	40
64.	PRAWN CURRY	41
65.	CRUSTED HALIBUT	41
66.	SHRIMP AND MUSHROOM RISOTTO	42
67.	HALIBUT SITKA	42
68.	AIR FRIED CALAMARI AND TOMATO PASTA	42
69.	AIR FRYER COCONUT SHRIMP	43
70.	AIR-FRIED SHRIMP	43
71.	AIR-FRIED SHRIMP	44
72.	GARLIC PARMESAN AIR FRIED SHRIMP RECIPE	44
73.	PARMESAN TILAPIA	45
74.	CHEESY BACON WRAPPED SHRIMP	45
75.	SALMON QUICHE	45
76.	AIR FRYER GARLIC SHRIMP WITH LEMON	46
77.	SHRIMP POKE	46

Air Fryer Meat Recipes 47

#	Title	Page
78.	PERFECT AIR FRYER STEAK: PALEO, WHOLE30, KETO, EASY!	47
79.	HOW TO MAKE STEAK IN THE AIR FRYER	47
80.	AIR FRYER MEATBALLS (LOW CARB)	48
81.	AIR FRYER ROAST BEEF	48
82.	AIR FRYER STUFFED PEPPERS	49
83.	AIR FRYER STEAK	49
84.	AIR FRYER STEAK FAJITAS	50
85.	AIR FRYER TACO CALZONES	51
86.	AIR FRYER STEAK BITES WITH MUSHROOMS	51
87.	AIR FRYER STEAK	52
88.	AIR FRYER ITALIAN-STYLE MEATBALLS	52
89.	AIR FRYER STEAK	53
90.	AIR FRYER STEAK BITES & MUSHROOMS	53

Air Fryer Vegetables Recipes 54

#	Title	Page
91.	AIR FRYER ROAST VEGETABLES	54
92.	AIR FRYER ROASTED BRUSSELS SPROUTS	54
93.	AIR FRYER ROASTED BROCCOLI (LOW CARB + KETO)	55
94.	AIR-FRYER ROASTED VEGGIES	55
95.	BUTTERY GARLIC GREEN BEANS	56
96.	SUPERB SAUTEED MUSHROOMS	56
97.	PAN-FRIED ASPARAGUS	57
98.	EASY ROASTED BROCCOLI	57
99.	AIR FRYER VEGGIES	57
100.	AIR FRYER "ROASTED" ASPARAGUS	58
101.	AIR FRYER VEGETABLES	58
102.	AIR FRYER FROZEN BROCCOLI, CARROTS, AND CAULIFLOWER – (GLUTEN-FREE, VEGAN, KETO, AND PALEO)	58
103.	HEALTHY AIR FRYER CHICKEN AND VEGGIES	59

Air Fryer Meatless Recipes 60

#	Title	Page
104.	GARLIC AND HERB ARTISAN BREAD	60
105.	SOY AND ONION SUGAR SNAP PEAS	60
106.	KOREAN BBQ CHICKPEAS	61
107.	AIR FRYER ROASTED ASPARAGUS	61
108.	EASY AIR FRYER BREAKFAST SCRUMBLED EGGS	62
109.	EASY ROASTED ASPARAGUS	62
110.	BLUEBERRY CREAM CHEESE CROISSANT BAKE	63

Air Fryer Pork And Beef Recipes 63

#	Title	Page
111.	MEATBALLS WITH GOCHUJANG MAYO	63
112.	GENERAL TSO'S PORK	64
113.	KOREAN MARINATED PORK BELLY	65
114.	KOREAN STYLE PORK CHOPS	65
115.	CHAR SIU PORK CHOPS	66
116.	WASABI LIME STEAK	66
117.	KOREAN BEEF WITH VEGGIE	66
118.	MONGOLIAN BEEF	67
119.	FIVE SPICES SALT AND PEPPER PORK	68

120.	SEASONED PORK CHOPS WITH AVOCADO SALSA.... 68
121.	CHINESE STYLE GROUND MEAT PATTIES 69
122.	PORK SATAY SKEWERS 69

Salad 70

123.	AIR FRYER BUFFALO SALMON SALAD 70
124.	GRILLED ROMAINE SALAD 70
125.	SESAME GINGER SALMON WITH SPICY CUCUMBER SALAD 71
126.	AIR FRYER SQUASH WITH KALE SALAD 71
127.	RADICCHIO SALAD WITH CASHEW RICOTTA DRESSING 73
128.	AIR FRYER CROUTONS 73
129.	GRILLED ROMAINE SALAD 74
130.	FRIED CHICKPEAS IN THE AIR FRYER 75
131.	AIR FRYER BUFFALO CHICKEN TENDERS SALAD 75

Seafood 76

132.	SEARED SCALLOPS WITH JALAPENO VINAIGRETTE .. 76
133.	BAKED TILAPIA WITH DILL SAUCE 77
134.	ANGY LEMON-GARLIC SHRIMP 77
135.	PARMESAN-CRUSTED SHRIMP SCAMPI WITH PASTA 78
136.	BEST TUNA CASSEROLE 78
137.	GOOD NEW ORLEANS CREOLE GUMBO 79
138.	SHRIMP SCAMPI WITH PASTA 80
139.	EASY GARLIC-LEMON SCALLOPS 80

Air Fryer Dessert And Snacks Recipes 81

140.	PEANUT BUTTER CUPCAKE SWIRL 81
141.	GLUTEN-FREE FRESH CHERRY CRUMBLE 81
142.	EASY AIR FRYER APPLE PIES 82
143.	CHOCOLATE CAKE IN AN AIR FRYER 82
144.	ZUCCHINI FRIES 83
145.	AIR FRYER SHORTBREAD COOKIE FRIES 84
146.	EASY AIR FRYER FRENCH TOAST STICKS 84
147.	AIR FRYER PEANUT BUTTER & JELLY S'MORES 85
148.	AIR FRYER APPLE CIDER DONUT BITES 85
149.	CHOCOLATE SPONGE CAKE 86

150.	RED BEAN WHEEL PIE 86
151.	SESAME CRUSTED SWEET POTATO CAKES 87
152.	STRAWBERRY PUFF PASTRY TWISTS 87
153.	MAPLE SPONGE CAKE 88
154.	ALMOND FLOUR CHOCOLATE BANANA NUT BROWNIE 88

Air fryer Healthy Recipes 89

155.	AIR FRYER GREEN BEANS 89
156.	HEALTHY AIR FRYER CHICKEN AND VEGGIES (20 MINUTES!) 89
157.	FRIED GREEN BEANS (AIR FRYER) 90
158.	AIR FRYER GREEN BEANS WITH BACON 90
159.	AIR FRYER STUFFED PEPPERS 91

What Is Air Frying?

First, a quick explanation of what air frying is and isn't. They don't fry food at all. They are more like a self-contained convection oven than a deep fat fryer. Most units have one or more heating elements, along with a fan or two to circulate the hot air. These appliances quickly heat and circulate the hot air around and through the food in the tray. This cooking method takes advantage of the heat and the drying effect of the air to cook foods quickly, leaving them crisp and browned on the outside but still moist inside. While the results can be similar to using a deep fryer, they are not identical.

Air Fryer Benefits

- An air fryer has many benefits to offer its customers.
- Low-fat meals
- Easy cleanup
- Uses hot-air circulation, the air fryer cooks your ingredients from all angles- with no oil needed.
- This ultimately produces healthier foods than most fryers and spares you from that unwanted aroma of fried foods in your home.
- To make sure you get the most out of your appliance, most fryers are accompanied by a recipe book to help you get started right away on your journey of fast, yet healthy meal preparations.
- Whether your favorite dish is french fries, muffins, chips, chicken tenders, or grilled vegetables, an air fryer can prepare it all.

Is an Air Fryer Useful?

At the tip of your fingers, you can have an appliance that specializes in making delicious, healthy meals that look and taste just like the ones made in oil fryers. The air fryer serves up many ways to be useful in your life.

Consider:

- Do you find yourself short on time to cook?
- Are you having a hard time letting go of those fatty foods, but still want to lose weight?
- Are you always seeking to get a bang for your buck?

If you answered yes to any of these questions, then an air fryer may be for you.

Why You Should Use An Air Fryer

An air fryer can pretty much do it all. And by all, we mean fry, grill, bake, and roast. Equipped with sturdy plastic and metal material, the air fryer has many great benefits to offer.

Air Fryers Can:

- Cook multiple dishes at once
- Cut back on fatty oils
- Prepare a meal within minutes
- While every appliance has its cons, the air fryer doesn't offer many.
- The fryer may be bulky in weight, but its dimensions are slimmer than most fryers. An air fryer can barely take up any counter space.
- If you need fast, healthy, convenient, and tasty, then once again, an air fryer may be for you.

Air Fryer- Healthier

The biggest quality the air fryer offers is healthier dishes

In comparison to other fryers, air fryers were designed to specifically function without fattening oils and to produce food with up to 80 percent less fat than food cooked with other fryers. The air fryer can help you lose the weight, you've been dying to get rid of. While it can be difficult to let go of your favorite fried foods, an air fryer will let you have your cake and eat it too. You can still have your fried dishes, but at the same time, still conserve those calories and saturated fat. The air fryer can also grill, bake, and roast foods as well. Offering you an all in one combination, the air fryer is the perfect appliance for anyone looking to switch to a healthier lifestyle.

Fast And Quick

- If you're on a tight schedule, you may want to use an air fryer.
- Within minutes you can have crunchy golden fries or crispy chicken tenders.
- This fryer is perfect for people who are constantly on the go and do not have much time to prepare meals.
- With most air fryers, french fries can be prepared within 12 minutes.
- That cuts the time you spend in the kitchen by a

tremendous amount.

Features

1. Temperature And Timer

- Avoid the waiting time for your fryer to decide when it wants to heat up.
- With an air fryer, once you power it on, the fryer will instantly heat.
- When using the appliance cold, that is, right after it has been off for a while (since last use) all you have to do is add three minutes to your cooking time to allow for it to heat up properly.
- The appliance is equipped with adjustable temperature control that allows you to set the temperature that can be altered for each of your meals.
- Most fryers can go up to 200-300 degrees.
- Because the fryer can cook food at record times, it comes with a timer that can be pre-set with no more than 30 minutes.
- You can even check on the progress of your foods without messing up the set time. Simply pull out the pan, and the fryer will cause heating. When you replace the pan, heating will resume.
- When your meal is prepared and your timer runs out, the fryer will alert you with its ready sound indicator. But just in-case you can't make it to the fryer when the timer goes, the fryer will automatically switch off to help prevent your ingredients from overcooking and burning.

2. Food Separator

Some air fryers are supplied with a food separator that enables you to prepare multiple meals at once. For example, if you wanted to prepare frozen chicken nuggets and french fries, you could use the separator to cook both ingredients at the same time, all the while avoiding the worry of the flavors mixing. An air fryer is perfect for quick and easy, lunch and dinner combinations. It is recommended to pair similar ingredients together when using the separator. This will allow both foods to share a similar temperature setting.

3. Air Filter

Some air fryers are built with an integrated air filter that eliminates those unwanted vapors and food odors from spreading around your house. No more smelling like your favorite fried foods, the air filter will diffuse that hot oil steam that floats and sticks. You can now enjoy your fresh kitchen smell before, during, and after using your air fryer.

4. Cleaning

- No need to fret after using an air fryer, it was designed for hassle-free cleaning.
- The parts of the fryer are constructed of non-stick material.
- This prevents any food from sticking to surfaces that ultimately make it hard to clean.
- It is recommended to soak the parts of the appliances before cleaning.
- All parts such as the grill, pan, and basket are removable and dishwasher friendly.
- After your ingredients are cooked to perfection, you can simply place your parts in the dishwasher for a quick and easy clean.

Tips On Cleaning An Air Fryer:

- Use detergent that specializes in dissolving oil.
- For a maximum and quick cleaning, leave the pan to soak in water and detergent for a few minutes.
- Avoid using metal utensils when cleaning the appliance to prevent scuffs and scratches on the material.
- Always let the fryer cool off for about 30 minutes before you wash it.

5. Cost-effective

Are there any cost-effective air fryers? For all that they can do, air fryers can be worth the cost. It has been highly questionable if the benefits of an air fryer are worth the expense. When you weigh your pros and cons, the air fryer surely leads with its pros. There aren't many fryers on the market that can fry, bake, grill and roast; and also promise you healthier meals. An air fryer saves you time, and could potentially save you money. Whether the air fryer is cost-effective for your life, is ultimately up to you.

The air fryer is a highly recommendable appliance to anyone starting a new diet, parents with busy schedules, or individuals who are always on the go. Deciding whether the investment is worth it, is all up to the purchaser. By weighing the air fryer advantages and the unique differences the air fryer has, compared to other fryers, you should be able to decide whether the air fryer has a lot to bring to the table.

Air Fryer Breakfast Recipes

1. EASY HARD BOILED EGGS

Cook Time: 16 minutes

Cooling: 5 minutes

Total Time: 21 minutes

Ingredients

- 6 large eggs You can use whatever size eggs you want and however many you want that will fit in the air fryer basket without stacking.

Instructions

- Place the eggs on the air fryer basket.
- Air fryer for 16 minutes at 260 degrees.
- Open the air fryer and remove the eggs. Place them in a bowl with ice and cold water.
- Allow the eggs to cool for 5 minutes.
- Peel and serve.

Nutrition Facts

- Calories: 72kcal | Protein: 6g | Fat: 5g

2. EASY CHERRY TURNOVERS

Prep Time: 15 minutes

Cook Time: 10 minutes

Total Time: 25 minutes

Ingredients

- 17 oz package puff pastry 4 sheets
- 10 oz can of cherry pie filling
- 1 egg beaten
- 2 tablespoons water
- cooking oil I use olive oil.

Instructions

- Lay the pastry sheets on a flat surface.
- Unfold both sheets of the puff pastry dough. Cut each sheet into 4 squares, making 8 squares total.
- Beat the egg in a small bowl along with the water to create an egg wash.
- Use a cooking brush or your fingers to brush along the edges of each square with the egg wash.
- Load 1 to 1 1/2 tablespoons of cherry pie filling into the middle of each square sheet. Do not overfill the pastry.
- Fold the dough over diagonally to create a triangle and seal the dough. Use the back of a fork to press lines into the open edges of each turnover to seal.
- Make 3 slits into the top of the crust to vent the turnovers.
- Brush the top of each turnover with the egg wash.
- Spritz the air fryer basket with cooking oil and

add the turnovers. Make sure they do not touch and do not stack the turnovers. Cook in batches if needed.
- Air fry at 370 degrees for 8 minutes. I did not flip.
- Allow the pastries to cool for 2-3 minutes before removing them from the air fryer.

Nutrition Facts
- Calories: 224kcal | Carbohydrates: 27g | Protein: 4g | Fat: 12g

3. TASTY BAKED EGGS

Preparation time: 10 minutes Cooking time: 20 minutes

Ingredients:
- 4 eggs
- 1 pound baby spinach, torn
- 7 ounces ham, chopped
- 4 tablespoons milk
- 1 tablespoon olive oil
- Cooking spray
- Salt and black pepper to the taste

Instructions:
- Heat up a pan with the oil over medium heat, add baby spinach, stir cook for a couple of minutes and take off heat.
- grease 4 ramekins with cooking spray and divide baby spinach and ham in each.
- Crack an egg in each ramekin, also divide milk, season with salt and pepper, place ramekins in preheated air fryer at 350 degrees F and bake for 20 minutes.
- Serve baked eggs for breakfast.

Nutrition Facts:

calories 321, fat 6, fiber 8, carbs 15, protein 12

4. BREAKFAST EGG BOWLS

Preparation time: 10 minutes Cooking time: 20 minutes

Ingredients:
- 4 dinner rolls, tops cut off and insides scooped out
- 4 tablespoons heavy cream
- 4 eggs
- 4 tablespoons mixed chives and parsley
- Salt and black pepper to the taste
- 4 tablespoons parmesan, grated

Instructions:
- Arrange dinner rolls on a baking sheet and crack an egg in each.
- Divide heavy cream, mixed herbs in each roll and season with salt and pepper.
- Sprinkle parmesan on top of your rolls, place them in your air fryer and cook at 350 degrees F for 20 minutes.
- Divide your bread bowls on plates and serve for breakfast.

Nutrition Facts:

calories 238, fat 4, fiber 7, carbs 14, protein 7

5. BLUEBERRY MUFFINS

Prep Time: 10 minutes

Cook Time: 15 minutes

Total Time: 25 minutes

Ingredients

- 1 1/2 cups all-purpose or white whole wheat flour
- 3/4 cup old-fashioned oats (oatmeal)
- 1/2 cup brown sweetener Light brown sugar can be used if preferred
- 1 tablespoon baking powder
- 1/2 teaspoon cinnamon
- 1/2 teaspoon salt
- 1 cup milk
- 1/4 cup melted unsalted butter (at room temperature)
- 2 eggs (at room temperature)
- 2 teaspoons vanilla
- 1 cup blueberries You can use fresh or frozen blueberries. If using frozen, do not thaw.

Instructions

- Combine the flour, rolled oats, salt, cinnamon, brown sweetener, and baking powder in a large mixing bowl. Mix.
- Combine the milk, eggs, vanilla, and butter in a separate medium-sized bowl. Mix using a silicone spoon.
- Add the wet ingredients to the dry ingredients in the mixing bowl. Stir.
- Fold in the blueberries and stir.
- Divide the batter among 12 silicone muffin cups and add them to the air fryer. Spraying the liners with oil is optional. The muffins generally don't stick.
- Place the air fryer at 350 degrees. Monitor the muffins closely for proper cook time, as every model will cook differently. The muffins will need to cook for 11-15 minutes. Insert a toothpick into the middle of a muffin, if it returns clean the muffins have finished baking. Mine was ready at about 13 minutes.

Nutrition Facts

- Calories: 121kcal | Carbohydrates: 13g | Protein: 3g | Fat: 5g

---

6. LOADED HASH BROWNS

Prep Time: 10 minutes

Cook Time: 20 minutes

Soak in water: 20 minutes

Total Time: 50 minutes

Ingredients

- 3 russet potatoes
- 1/4 cup chopped green peppers
- 1/4 cup chopped red peppers
- 1/4 cup chopped onions
- 2 garlic cloves chopped
- 1 teaspoon paprika
- salt and pepper to taste
- 2 teaspoons olive oil

Instructions

- Grate the potatoes using the largest holes of a cheese grater.
- Place the potatoes in a bowl of cold water. Allow the potatoes to soak for 20-25 minutes. Soaking the potatoes in cold water will help remove the starch from the potatoes. This makes them crunchy.
- Drain the water from the potatoes and dry them completely using a paper towel.
- Place the potatoes in a dry bowl. Add the garlic, paprika, olive oil, and salt and pepper to taste. Stir to combine the ingredients.
- Add the potatoes to the air fryer.
- Cook for ten minutes at 400 degrees.
- Open the air fryer and shake the potatoes.
- Add the chopped peppers and onions. Cook for an additional ten minutes.
- Cool before serving.

Nutrition Facts

- Calories: 246kcal | Carbohydrates: 42g | Protein: 6g | Fat: 3g

7. AIR FRYER SAUSAGE BREAKFAST CASSEROLE

Prep Time: 10 Minutes

Cook Time: 20 Minutes

Total Time: 30 Minutes

Ingredients

- 1 Lb Hash Browns
- 1 Lb Ground Breakfast Sausage
- 1 Green Bell Pepper Diced
- 1 Red Bell Pepper Diced
- 1 Yellow Bell Pepper Diced
- 1/4 Cup Sweet Onion Diced
- 4 Eggs

Instructions

- Foil line the basket of your air fryer.
- Place the hash browns on the bottom.
- Top it with the uncooked sausage.
- Evenly place the peppers and onions on top.
- Cook on 355* for 10 minutes.
- Open the air fryer and mix up the casserole a bit if needed.
- Crack each egg in a bowl, then pour right on top of the casserole.
- Cook on 355* for another 10 minutes.
- Serve with salt and pepper to taste.

Nutrition Information

- Calories:517|Totalfat:37g|Saturatedfat:10g|Transfat:0g|Cholesterol:227mg|Sodium: 1092mg|Carbohydrates:27g|Sugar: 4g|Protein: 21g

8. AIR FRYER BAKED EGG CUPS W/ SPINACH & CHEESE

Prep Time: 5 mins

Cook Time: 10 mins

Total Time: 15 mins

Ingredients

- 1 large egg
- 1 tablespoon (15 ml) milk or half & half
- 1 tablespoon (15 ml) frozen spinach, thawed (or sautéed fresh spinach)
- 1-2 teaspoons (5 ml) grated cheese
- Salt, to taste
- Black pepper, to taste
- Cooking spray, for muffin cups or ramekins

Instructions

- Spray inside of silicone muffin cups or ramekin with oil spray.
- Add egg, milk, spinach, and cheese into the muffin cup or ramekin.
- Season with salt and pepper. Gently stir ingredients into egg whites without breaking the yolk.
- Air Fry at 330°F for about 6-12 minutes (single egg cups usually take about 6 minutes - multiple or doubled up cups take as much as 12. As you add more egg cups, you will need to add more time.)
- Cooking in a ceramic ramekin may take a little longer. If you want runny yolks, cook for less time. Keep checking the eggs after 5 minutes to ensure the egg is to your preferred texture.

Nutrition Facts

- Calories: 115kcal | Carbohydrates: 1g | Protein: 10g | Fat: 7g | Saturated Fat: 2g | Cholesterol: 216mg | Sodium: 173mg | Potassium: 129mg | Sugar: 1g | Vitamin A: 2040IU | Calcium: 123mg | Iron: 1.3mg

9. AIRFRYER FRENCH TOAST STICKS RECIPE

Prep Time: 5 minutes

Cook Time: 12 minutes

Total Time: 17 minutes

Ingredients

- 4 pieces bread (whatever kind and thickness desired)
- 2 Tbsp butter (or margarine, softened)
- 2 eggs (gently beaten)
- 1 pinch salt
- 1 pinch cinnamon
- 1 pinch nutmeg
- 1 pinch ground cloves
- 1 tsp icing sugar (and/or maple syrup for garnish and serving)

Instructions

- Preheat Airfryer to 180* Celsius.
- In a bowl, gently beat together two eggs, a sprinkle of salt, a few heavy shakes of cinnamon, and small pinches of both nutmeg and ground cloves.
- Butter both sides of bread slices and cut into strips.
- Dredge each strip in the egg mixture and arrange it in Airfryer (you will have to cook in two batches).
- After 2 minutes of cooking, pause the Airfryer, take out the pan, making sure you place the pan on a heat-safe surface and spray the bread with cooking spray.
- Once you have generously coated the strips, flip and spray the second side as well.
- Return pan to the fryer and cook for 4 more minutes, checking after a couple of minutes to ensure they are cooking evenly and not burning.
- When the egg is cooked and the bread is golden brown, remove it from Airfryer and serve immediately.
- To garnish and serve, sprinkle with icing sugar, top with whip cream, drizzle with maple syrup, or serve with a small bowl of syrup for dipping.

Nutrition Facts

- Calories:178Kcal|Totalfat:15g|Saturatedfat:8g| Transfat:12g|Cholesterol:194mg|Sodium: 193mg|Carbohydrates: 2g|Sugar: 1g|Protein: 5g| Iron: 0.8mg| Calcium: 25mg

10. AIR FRYER BREAKFAST FRITTATA

Prep Time: 15 mins

Cook Time: 20 mins

Total Time: 35 mins

Ingredients

- ¼ pound breakfast sausage fully cooked and crumbled
- 4 eggs, lightly beaten
- ½ cup shredded Cheddar-Monterey Jack cheese blend
- 2 tablespoons red bell pepper, diced
- 1 green onion, chopped
- 1 pinch cayenne pepper (Optional)
- cooking spray

Direction

- Combine sausage, eggs, Cheddar-Monterey Jack cheese, bell pepper. onion, and cayenne in a bowl and mix to combine.
- Preheat the air fryer to 360 degrees F (180 degrees C). Spray a nonstick 6x2-inch cake pan with cooking spray.
- Place egg mixture in the prepared cake pan.

- Cook in the air fryer until frittata is set, 18 to 20 minutes.

Nutrition Facts

Calories: 380| Protein 31.2g| Carbohydrates 2.9g| Fat 27.4g| Cholesterol 443mg| Sodium 693.5mg| Vitamin A Iu: 894.6IU|Vitamin B6: 0.3mg|Vitamin C: 13.4mg|Calcium:69.2mg|Iron:3mg|Magnesium:26.7mg|Potassium:328.4mg| Sodium: 693.5mg|Thiamin: 0.1mg

11. BREAKFAST POTATOES IN THE AIR FRYER

Prep Time: 2 minutes

Cook Time: 15 minutes

Total Time: 17 minutes

Servings: 2

Ingredients

- 5 medium potatoes, peeled and cut to 1-inch cubes (Yukon Gold works best)
- 1 tbsp oil
- Breakfast Potato Seasoning
- 1/2 tsp kosher salt
- 1/2 tsp smoked paprika
- 1/2 tsp garlic powder
- 1/4 tsp black ground pepper

Instructions

- Preheat the air fryer for about 2-3 minutes at 400F degrees. This will give you the crispiest potatoes.
- Meanwhile, toss the potatoes with breakfast potato seasoning and oil until thoroughly coated.
- Spray the air fryer basket with a nonstick spray. Add the potatoes and cook for about 15 minutes, stopping and shaking the basket 2-3 times throughout to promote even cooking.
- Transfer to a plate and serve right away.

Nutrition Facts

- Calories: 375 Fat: 7g odium: 635mg Potassium: 2199mg63 Carbohydrates: 67g Fiber: 13 Protein: 13g

Air Fryer Side Dishes & Dinner Recipes

12. 3 INGREDIENT FRIED CATFISH

Prep Time5 minutes

Cook Time: 20 minutes

Total Time: 25 minutes

Ingredients

- 4 catfish fillets
- 1/4 cup Louisiana Fish Fry Coating
- 1 tbsp olive oil
- 1 tbsp chopped parsley optional

Instructions

- Pat the catfish dry.
- Sprinkle the fish fry onto both sides of each fillet. Ensure the entire filet is coated with seasoning.
- Spritz olive oil on the top of each filet.
- Place the filet in the Air Fryer basket. Do not stack the fish and do not overcrowd the basket. Cook in batches if needed. Close and cook for 10 minutes at 400 degrees.

- Open the air fryer and flip the fish. Cook for an additional 10 minutes.
- Open and flip the fish.
- Cook for an additional 2-3 minutes or until desired crispness.
- Top with optional parsley.

Nutrition Facts

- Calories: 208kcal | Carbohydrates: 8g | Protein: 17g | Fat: 9g

13. BANG BANG FRIED SHRIMP

Prep Time: 10 minutes

Cook Time: 20 minutes

Total Time: 30 minutes

Ingredients

- 1 pound raw shrimp peeled and deveined
- 1 egg white 3 tbsp
- 1/2 cup all-purpose flour
- 3/4 cup panko bread crumbs
- 1 tsp paprika
- Mccormick's grill mates montreal chicken seasoning to taste
- Salt and pepper to taste
- Cooking oil

Bang Bang Sauce

- 1/3 cup plain, non-fat Greek yogurt
- 2 tbsp Sriracha
- 1/4 cup sweet chili sauce

Instructions

- Preheat Air Fryer to 400 degrees.
- Season the shrimp with the seasonings.
- Place the flour, egg whites, and panko bread crumbs in three separate bowls.
- Create a cooking station. Dip the shrimp in the flour, then the egg whites, and the panko bread crumbs last.
- When dipping the shrimp in the egg whites, you do not need to submerge the shrimp. Do a light dab so that most of the flour stays on the shrimp. You want the egg white to adhere to the panko crumbs.
- Spray the shrimp with cooking oil.
- Add the shrimp to the Air Fryer basket. Cook for 4 minutes. Open the basket and flip the shrimp to the other side. Cook for an additional 4 minutes or until crisp.

Bang Bang Sauce

- Combine all of the ingredients in a small bowl. Mix thoroughly to combine.

Nutrition Facts

- Calories: 242kcal | Carbohydrates: 32g | Protein: 37g | Fat: 1g

14. FRIED SHRIMP SANDWICH RECIPE

Prep Time: 20 minutes

Cook Time: 10 minutes

Total Time: 30 minutes

Ingredients

- 1 pound shrimp, deveined
- 1 teaspoon creole seasoning i used tony chachere
- 1/4 cup buttermilk
- 1/2 cup louisiana fish fry coating
- Cooking oil spray (if air frying) i use olive oil
- Canola or vegetable oil (if pan-frying) you will need enough oil to fill 2 inches of height in your frying pan.
- 4 french bread hoagie rolls i used 2 loaves, cut each in half
- 2 cups shredded iceberg lettuce
- 8 tomato slices

Remoulade Sauce

- 1/2 cup mayo I used reduced-fat 1 tsp minced garlic
- 1/2 lemon juice of
- 1 tsp Worcestershire
- 1/2 tsp Creole Seasoning I used Tony Chachere
- 1 tsp Dijon mustard
- 1 tsp hot sauce
- 1 green onion chopped

Instructions

Remoulade Sauce

- Combine all of the ingredients in a small bowl. Refrigerate before serving while the shrimp cooks.

Shrimp And Breading

- Marinate the shrimp in the Creole seasoning and buttermilk for 30 minutes. I like to use a sealable plastic bag to do this.
- Add the fish fry to a bowl. Remove the shrimp from the bags and dip each into the fish fry. Add the shrimp to the air fryer basket.

Pan Fry

- Heat a frying pan with 2 inches of oil to 350 degrees. Use a thermometer to test the heat.
- Fry the shrimp on both sides for 3-4 minutes until crisp.
- Remove the shrimp from the pan and drain the excess grease using paper towels.

Air Fryer

- Spray the air fryer basket with cooking oil. Add the shrimp to the air fryer basket.
- Spritz the shrimp with cooking oil.
- Cook the shrimp for 5 minutes at 400 degrees. Open the basket and flip the shrimp to the other side. Cook for an additional 3-5 minutes or until crisp.
- Assemble the Po Boy
- Spread the remoulade sauce on the French bread.
- Add the sliced tomato and lettuce, and then the shrimp.

Nutritional Facts

- Serving: 1serving | Calories: 437kcal | Carbohydrates: 55g | Protein: 24g | Fat: 12g

15. EASY ROASTED WHOLE CHICKEN

Prep Time: 15 minutes

Cook Time: 55 minutes

Resting: 15 minutes

Total Time: 1 hour 25 minutes

Ingredients

- 1 4.5-5 pounds whole chicken
- 1/2 fresh lemon
- 1/4 whole onion
- 4 sprigs of fresh thyme
- 4 sprigs of fresh rosemary
- Olive oil spray

- 1 teaspoon ground thyme i like to use ground thyme in addition to fresh thyme for optimal flavor.
- 1 teaspoon onion powder
- 1 teaspoon garlic powder
- Kosher salt to taste be sure to use kosher salt.

Instructions

- I purchased my whole chicken ready with the contents of the cavity removed. If your chicken still has the giblets inside of it, you will need to remove them before cooking.
- Stuff 1/2 of fresh-cut lemon and 1/4 of a chopped onion inside the cavity of the chicken along with the fresh rosemary and thyme.
- Make sure the chicken is completely dry on the outside. Pat dry with paper towels if necessary. A dry chicken will help it crisp in the air fryer with the olive oil.
- Spray olive oil onto both sides of the chicken using an oil sprayer.
- Sprinkle the seasonings throughout and onto both sides of the chicken. You may elect to only season the bottom side of the chicken at this step. Because you will need to flip the chicken during the air frying process, you will likely lose some of the seasonings at this stage. My preference is to season both sides initially, and then re-assess if more seasoning (usually salt is needed later).
- Line the air fryer with parchment paper. This makes for easy cleanup. Load the chicken into the air fryer basket with the breast side down.
- Air fry the chicken for 30 minutes at 330 degrees.
- Open the air fryer and flip the chicken. I gripped the chicken cavity with tongs to flip.
- Re-assess if more seasoning is needed on the breasts, legs, and wings. Add additional if necessary.
- Air fry for an additional 20-25 minutes until the chicken reaches an internal temperature of 165 degrees. Use a meat thermometer.
- This step is important. Place the meat thermometer in the thickest part of the chicken, which is typically the chicken thigh area. I like to test the breast too, just to ensure the entire chicken is fully cooked.
- Remove the chicken from the air fryer basket and place it on a plate to rest for at least 15 minutes before cutting into the chicken. This will allow the moisture to redistribute throughout the chicken before you cut into it.

Nutrition Facts

- Calories: 340kcal | Carbohydrates: 2g | Protein: 33g | Fat: 22g

16. BEEF TACO FRIED EGG ROLLS

Prep Time: 15 minutes

Cook Time: 25 minutes

Total Time: 40 minutes

Servings: 8

Ingredients

- 1 pound ground beef
- 16 egg roll wrappers i used wing hing brand
- 1/2 cup chopped onion i used red onion.
- 2 garlic cloves minced
- 16 oz can diced tomatoes and chilies i used mexican rotel.
- 8 oz refried black beans i used fat-free and 1/2 of a 16oz can.
- 1 cup shredded mexican cheese
- 1/2 cup whole kernel corn i used frozen
- Cooking oil spray
- Homemade taco seasoning
- 1 tablespoon chili powder
- 1 teaspoon cumin
- 1 teaspoon smoked paprika
- Salt and pepper to taste

Instructions

- Add the ground beef to a skillet on medium-high heat along with the salt, pepper, and taco seasoning. Cook until browned while breaking the beef into smaller chunks.
- Once the meat has started to brown add the chopped onions and garlic. Cook until the onions become fragrant.
- Add the diced tomatoes and chilis, Mexican cheese, beans, and corn. Stir to ensure the mixture is combined.
- Lay the egg roll wrappers on a flat surface. Dip a cooking brush in water. Glaze each of the egg

roll wrappers with the wet brush along the edges. This will soften the crust and make it easier to roll.
- Load 2 tablespoons of the mixture into each of the wrappers. Do not overstuff. Depending on the brand of egg roll wrappers you use, you may need to double wrap the egg rolls.
- Fold the wrappers diagonally to close. Press firmly on the area with the filling, cup it to secure it in place. Fold in the left and right sides as triangles. Fold the final layer over the top to close. Use the cooking brush to wet the area and secure it in place.
- Spray the air fryer basket with cooking oil.
- Load the egg rolls into the basket of the Air Fryer. Spray each egg roll with cooking oil.
- Cook for 8 minutes at 400 degrees. Flip the egg rolls. Cook for an additional 4 minutes or until browned and crisp.

Nutrition Facts

Calories: 348kcal | Carbohydrates: 38g | Protein: 24g | Fat: 11g

17. PARMESAN TRUFFLE OIL FRIES

Prep Time 10 minutes

Cook Time 40 minutes

Total Time 50 minutes

Ingredients

- 3 large russet potatoes peeled and cut lengthwise
- 2 tbsp white truffle oil
- 2 tbsp parmesan shredded
- 1 tsp paprika
- salt and pepper to taste
- 1 tbsp parsley chopped

Instructions

- Place the sliced potatoes in a large bowl with cold water.
- Allow the potatoes to soak in the water for at least 30 minutes, preferably an hour.
- Spread the fries onto a flat surface and dry them completely with paper towels. Coat them with 1 tbsp of the white truffle oil and seasonings.
- Add half of the fries to the Air Fryer basket. Adjust the temperature to 380 degrees and cook for 15-20 minutes. Set a timer for 10 minutes and stop and shake the basket at the 10-minute mark (once).
- Use your judgment. If the fries need to be crisper, allow them to cook for additional time. If the fries look crisp before 15 minutes, remove them. I cooked both of my batches for almost 20 minutes.
- When the first half finishes, cook the remaining half.
- Add the remaining truffle oil and parmesan to the fries immediately upon removing them from the Air Fryer.
- Top with shredded parsley. Serve!

Nutrition Facts

- Calories: 233kcal

18. LOW-FAT WEIGHT WATCHERS MOZZARELLA CHEESE STICKS

Prep Time: 10 minutes

ook Time: 16 minutes

Ingredients

- 10 pieces mozzarella string cheese I used Weight Watchers Smoked Flavor
- 1 cup Italian breadcrumbs
- 1 egg
- 1/2 cup flour
- 1 cup marinara sauce
- Salt and pepper to taste

Instructions

- Season the breadcrumbs with salt and pepper.
- Create a workstation by adding the flour, bread crumbs, and eggs to separate bowls.
- Dip each string of cheese in flour, then egg, and last the breadcrumbs.
- Freeze the sticks for one hour so that they harden. This will help the cheese maintain the stick shape while frying.
- Season your Air Fryer basket before each use so that items do not stick. I like to glaze the basket with coconut oil using a cooking brush.
- Turn the Air Fryer on 400 degrees. Add the sticks to the fryer.
- Cook for 8 minutes. Remove the basket. Flip each stick. You can use tongs, but be careful not to manipulate the shape. I used my hands to flip them. They weren't too hot. Cook for an additional 8 minutes.
- Allow the sticks to cool for 5 minutes before removing them from the pan. Some of the sticks may leak cheese on the outside. Allow the sticks to cool, and then use your hands to correct the shape.

Nutrition Facts

- Calories: 224kcal | Carbohydrates: 19g | Protein: 17g | Fat: 7g

19. CARROTS (THREE WAYS)

Prep Time: 5 minutes

Cook Time: 20 minutes

Total Time: 25 minutes

Ingredients

- 4 cups sliced carrots (1/4-inch thick), washed and patted dry
- 2 tablespoons extra virgin olive oil

Savory Version

- 1/2 teaspoon garlic powder
- 1/2 teaspoon dried basil
- 1/2 teaspoon dried oregano
- 1/2 teaspoon dried parsley
- 1/2 teaspoon kosher salt
- 1/4 teaspoon ground black pepper

Sweet Version

- 1 tablespoon coconut sugar
- 1/2 tablespoon maple syrup
- 1/4 teaspoon kosher salt
- 1/8 teaspoon crushed red pepper flakes

Spicy Version

- 1 teaspoon ground cumin
- 1 teaspoon smoked paprika
- 1/2 teaspoon kosher salt
- 1/8 teaspoon cayenne pepper
- 1/8 teaspoon ground black pepper

Instructions

- Add the sliced carrots to a large bowl and evenly coat with oil. Add your choice of

seasonings and toss to coat.
- Place carrots in the air fryer basket and air fry on 400F for 18-20 minutes, or until fork-tender. Shake or stir the carrots after about 10 minutes. Serve immediately.

Nutritional Facts
- Total Fat: 7.3g Total Carbohydrate: 12.2g Sugar: 5.8g alcium: 45.9mg Sat Fat: 1.1g Sodium: 239.8mg Fiber: 3.6g Protein: 1.3g Vitamin C: 7.3mg Iron: 0.5g

20. BUTTERNUT SQUASH (HOME FRIES)

Prep Time: 10 minutes

Cook Time: 20 minutes

Total Time: 30 minutes

Ingredients
- 4 cups chopped butternut squash, 1-inch cubes (see cutting tips above)
- 2 tablespoons extra virgin olive oil
- 1 tablespoon maple syrup
- 1 teaspoon dried oregano
- 1/2 teaspoon garlic powder
- 1/2 teaspoon smoked paprika
- 1/2 teaspoon kosher salt
- 1/4 teaspoon ground chipotle chili pepper

Instructions
- In a large bowl, add the squash cubes along with the other ingredients. Toss until the cubes are well coated.
- Arrange the cubes in a single layer in the air fryer basket and air fry on 400F for 15-20 minutes, or until the squash is fork-tender and a little crispy on the outside. Shake or stir the cubes at the mid-way point.
- Carefully remove from the air fryer and serve immediately.

Nutritional Facts
- Calories: 140 Total Fat: 7.2g otal Carbohydrate: 20.5g Sugar: 6.2g Calcium: 81.2mg Sat Fat: 1g Sodium: 302.3mg Fiber: 3.2g Protein: 1.6g Vitamin C: 29.4mg Iron: 1.3g

Air Fryer Main & Lunch Recipes

21. SEXY AIR-FRIED MEATLOAF

Prep Time: 10 mins

Cook Time: 45 mins

Additional Time: 1 day

Total Time: 1 day

Ingredient
- ½ pound ground pork
- ½ pound ground veal
- 1 large egg
- ¼ cup chopped fresh cilantro
- ¼ cup gluten-free bread crumbs
- 2 medium spring onions, diced
- ½ teaspoon ground black pepper
- ½ teaspoon Sriracha salt
- ½ cup ketchup
- 2 teaspoons gluten-free chipotle chili sauce
- 1 teaspoon olive oil
- 1 teaspoon blackstrap molasses

Instructions
- Preheat the air fryer to 400 degrees F (200 degrees C).
- Combine pork and veal in a nonstick baking dish that fits inside the air fryer basket. Make a well and add egg, cilantro, bread crumbs, spring onions, black pepper, and 1/2 teaspoon of Sriracha salt. Mix well using your hands. Form a loaf inside the baking dish.
- Combine ketchup, chipotle chili sauce, olive oil,

and molasses in a small bowl and whisk well. Set aside, but do not refrigerate.
- Cook meatloaf in the air fryer for 25 minutes without opening the basket. Remove meatloaf and top with ketchup mixture, covering the top completely. Return meatloaf to air fryer and bake until internal temperature reaches 160 degrees F (71 degrees C), about 7 minutes more.
- Turn off the air fryer and let the meatloaf rest inside for 5 minutes. Take the meatloaf out and let rest 5 minutes more before slicing and serving.

Nutrition Facts

- Calories: 272; Protein 22.1g; Carbohydrates 13.3g; Fat 14.4g; Cholesterol 123.5mg; Sodium 536.1mg.

22. HAM AND MOZZARELLA EGGPLANT BOATS

Prep Time: 17 minutes

Ingredients

- 1 eggplant
- 4 ham slices, chopped
- 1 cup shredded mozzarella cheese, divided
- 1 tsp. dried parsley
- Salt and pepper, to taste

Instructions

- Preheat the air fryer to 330 degrees.
- Peel the eggplant and cut it lengthwise in half. Scoop some of the flash out. Season with salt and pepper.
- Divide half the mozzarella cheese between the eggplants.
- Place the ham on top of the mozzarella.
- Top with the remaining mozzarella cheese.
- Sprinkle with parsley. Cook 12 minutes

Nutrition Facts

Calories 323.1, Carbohydrates 15.7 g, Fat 16.4 g, Protein 28.3 g

23. LEFTOVER TURKEY AND MUSHROOM SANDWICH

Prep Time: 15 MInutes

Ingredients

- 1/3 cup shredded leftover turkey
- 1/3 cup sliced mushrooms
- 1 tbsp. butter, divided
- 2 tomato slices
- ½ tsp. red pepper flakes
- ¼ tsp. salt
- ¼ tsp. black pepper
- 1 hamburger bun

Instructions

- Preheat the air fryer to 350 degrees F.
- Melt half of the butter and add the mushrooms.
- Cook for about 4 minutes.
- Meanwhile, cut the bun in half and spread the remaining butter on the outside of the bun.
- Place the turkey on one half of the bun. Arrange the mushroom slices on top of the turkey. Place the tomato slices on top of the mushrooms.
- Sprinkle with salt pepper and red pepper flakes. Top with the other bun half. Cook for 5 minutes.

Nutrition Facts

Calories 318.3, Carbohydrates 25.6 g, Fat 16.4 g, Protein 18.4 g

24. ITALIAN SAUSAGE PATTIES

Prep Time: 20 Minutes

Ingredients

- 1 lb. ground Italian sausage
- ¼ cup breadcrumbs
- 1 tsp. dried parsley
- 1 tsp. red pepper Flakes
- ½ tsp. salt
- ¼ tsp. black peppe
- r¼ tsp. garlic powder
- 1 egg, beaten

Instructions

- Preheat the air fryer to 350 degrees F.
- Combine all of the **Ingredients** in a large bowl.Line a baking sheet with parchment paper.
- Make patties out of the sausage mixture and arrange them on the baking sheet.Cook for about 15 minutes.
- Serve as desired (they are amazing with tzatziki sauce)

Nutrition Facts

Calories 332.3 Carbohydrates 6.2 g, Fat 24.6 g, Protein 18.6 g

25. AIR-FRIED POPCORN CHICKEN GIZZARDS

Prep Time: 10 mins Cook Time: 45 mins Additional Time: 5 mins Total Time: 1 hr

Ingredient

- 1 pound chicken gizzards
- ⅓ cup all-purpose flour
- 1 ½ teaspoon seasoned salt
- ½ teaspoon ground black pepper
- ½ teaspoon garlic powder
- ½ teaspoon paprika
- 1 pinch cayenne pepper (optional)
- 1 large egg, beaten
- Cooking spray

Instructions

- Bring a large pot of water to a boil. Cut gizzards into bite-sized pieces and add to the boiling water. Boil for 30 minutes. Drain.
- Combine flour, seasoned salt, pepper, garlic powder, paprika, and cayenne in a flat plastic container. Snap the lid on and shake until combined.
- Add gizzards to the seasoned flour. Snap the lid back on and shake until evenly coated.
- Place beaten egg in a separate bowl. Dip each gizzard piece into the beaten egg and then place it back in the seasoned flour. Snap the lid on and shake one last time. Let sit for 5 minutes while the air fryer preheats.
- Preheat the air fryer to 400 degrees F (200 degrees C).
- Place gizzards in the basket and spray the tops with cooking spray. Cook for 4 minutes. Shake the basket and spray any chalky spots with more cooking spray. Cook for 4 minutes more.

Nutrition Facts

- Calories: 237; Protein 23.6g; Carbohydrates 11.8g; Fat 10g; Cholesterol 330.8mg; Sodium 434.2mg

26. AIR FRYER CRAB RANGOON

Prep Time: 15 mins Cook Time: 20 mins Total Time: 35 mins

Ingredient

- 1 (8 ounces) package cream cheese, softened
- 4 ounces lump crab meat
- 2 tablespoons chopped scallions
- 1 teaspoon soy sauce
- 1 teaspoon Worcestershire sauce
- 1 serving nonstick cooking spray
- 24 each wonton wrappers
- 2 tablespoons Asian sweet chili sauce, for dipping

Instructions

- Combine cream cheese, crab meat, scallions, soy sauce, and Worcestershire sauce in a bowl; stir until evenly combined.
- Preheat an air fryer to 350 degrees F (175 degrees C). Spray the basket of the air fryer with cooking spray. Fill a small bowl with warm water.
- Place 12 wonton wrappers on a clean work surface. Spoon 1 teaspoon of cream cheese mixture into the center of each wonton wrapper. Dip index finger into the warm water and wet around the sides of each wonton wrapper. Crimp wrapper corners upwards to meet in the center to form dumplings.
- Place dumplings in the prepared basket and spray the tops with cooking spray.
- Cook dumplings until desired crispness, about 8 to 10 minutes. Transfer to a paper towel-lined plate.
- While the first batch is cooking, assemble the remaining dumplings with the remaining wrappers and filling.
- Serve with sweet chili sauce for dipping.

Nutrition Facts

- Calories: 127; Protein 5.1g; Carbohydrates 11.1g; Fat 6.9g; Cholesterol 29.1mg; Sodium 240.4mg.

27. AIR FRYER CAULIFLOWER FRIED RICE

Prep Time: 5 mins

Cook Time: 10 mins

Total Time: 15 mins

Ingredient

- 1 (12 ounces) package frozen cauliflower rice
- 2 large eggs
- 2 slices deli ham
- ¼ cup chopped green onions
- 2 tablespoons soy sauce

Instructions

- Cook cauliflower rice in the microwave for 5 to 6 minutes. Let stand for 1 minute before carefully opening the bag.
- Preheat the air fryer to 400 degrees F (200 degrees C). Cover the bottom and 1/2 inch of the basket sides with aluminum foil.
- Mix cauliflower rice, eggs, ham, green onions, and soy sauce in a bowl until well combined.
- Air fry for 5 minutes. Remove the basket and stir the cauliflower mixture. Return to air fryer and cook for an additional 5 minutes.

Nutrition Facts

- Calories: 170; Protein 16.2g; Carbohydrates 11.6g; Fat 7.4g; Cholesterol 202mg; Sodium 1379mg.

28. AIR FRYER WIENER SCHNITZEL

Prep Time: 10 mins Cook Time: 20 mins

Total Time: 30 mins

Ingredient

- 1 pound veal, scallopini cut
- 2 tablespoons lemon juice
- salt and ground black pepper to taste
- ¼ cup all-purpose flour
- 1 egg
- 1 tablespoon chopped fresh parsley
- 1 cup panko bread crumbs
- nonstick cooking spray
- 1 lemon, cut into wedges

Instructions

- Preheat an air fryer to 400 degrees F (200 degrees C).
- Place veal on a clean work surface and sprinkle with lemon juice, salt, and pepper.
- Place flour in a flat dish. Beat egg and parsley together in a second dish. Place bread crumbs in a third dish. Dredge each veal cutlet first in flour, then in the egg-parsley mixture, followed by bread crumbs, pressing down so that bread crumbs adhere.
- Spray the basket of the air fryer with nonstick cooking spray. Place breaded veal cutlets into the basket, making sure not to overcrowd. Spray the tops with nonstick cooking spray.
- Cook for 5 minutes. Flip, spray any chalky spots with nonstick cooking spray and cook for 5 minutes longer. Repeat with remaining veal. Serve with lemon wedges.

Nutrition Facts

- Calories: 215; Protein 18g; Carbohydrates 28.4g; Fat 6.6g; Cholesterol 104.4mg; Sodium 239.3mg.

29. AIR FRYER STEAK AND CHEESE MELTS

Prep Time: 10 mins

Cook Time: 25 mins

Additional Time: 4 hrs 30 mins

Total Time: 5 hrs 5 mins

Ingredient

- 1 pound beef rib-eye steak, thinly sliced
- 2 tablespoons Worcestershire sauce
- 1 tablespoon reduced-sodium soy sauce
- 1 medium onion, sliced into petals
- 4 ounces sliced baby portobello mushrooms
- ½ green bell pepper, thinly sliced
- 1 tablespoon olive oil
- ½ teaspoon salt
- ½ teaspoon ground mustard
- ¼ teaspoon ground black pepper
- 4 hoagie rolls
- 4 slices Provolone cheese

Instructions

- Place steak in a bowl and add Worcestershire and soy sauce. Cover and refrigerate 4 hours to overnight. Remove from the refrigerator and let come to room temperature, about 30 minutes.
- Preheat the air fryer to 380 degrees F (190 degrees C).

- Combine onion, mushrooms, and bell pepper in a large bowl. Add olive oil, salt, ground mustard, and pepper; stir to coat.
- Place hoagie rolls in the basket of the air fryer and cook until toasted, about 2 minutes. Transfer rolls to a plate.
- Place steak in the basket of the air fryer and cook for 3 minutes. Stir and cook for 1 more minute. Transfer to a plate.
- Add vegetable mix to the basket of the air fryer and cook for 5 minutes. Stir and cook until softened, about 5 more minutes.
- Stir steak into the vegetable mixture. Place cheese slices on top, slightly overlapping. Cook until cheese is melted and bubbly, about 3 minutes. Spoon mixture onto toasted rolls and serve immediately.

Nutrition Facts

- Calories: 679; Protein 33.4g; Carbohydrates 75.4g; Fat 26.4g; Cholesterol 81.9mg; Sodium 1540.8mg.

30. AIR FRYER SALMON FOR ONE

Prep Time: 5 mins

Cook Time: 15 mins

Total Time: 20 mins

Ingredient

- 1 (6 ounces) salmon fillet
- ½ teaspoon salt
- ½ teaspoon Greek seasoning (such as Cavender's®)
- ¼ teaspoon ground black pepper
- 1 pinch dried dill weed

Instructions

- Preheat the air fryer to 370 degrees F (190 degrees C) for 5 minutes.
- Meanwhile, season salmon fillet with salt, Greek seasoning, pepper, and dill.
- Line the inner basket of the air fryer with a perforated parchment round. Place salmon onto the parchment, skin side down.
- Air fry salmon until salmon is cooked through, about 15 minutes.

Nutrition Facts

- Calories: 189; Protein 31.1g; Carbohydrates 1.5g; Fat 5.8g; Cholesterol 72mg; Sodium 1478mg.

31. EASY AIR FRYER FRENCH TOAST STICKS

Prep Time: 10 mins

Cook Time: 10 mins

Total Time: 20 mins

Ingredient

- 4 slices of slightly stale thick bread, such as Texas toast
- Parchment paper
- 2 eggs, lightly beaten
- ¼ cup milk
- 1 teaspoon vanilla extract
- 1 teaspoon cinnamon
- 1 pinch ground nutmeg (optional)

Instructions

- Cut each slice of bread into thirds to make sticks. Cut a piece of parchment paper to fit the bottom of the air fryer basket.
- Preheat air fryer to 360 degrees F (180 degrees C).
- Stir together eggs, milk, vanilla extract, cinnamon, and nutmeg in a bowl until well combined. Dip each piece of bread into the egg mixture, making sure each piece is well submerged. Shake each breadstick to remove excess liquid and place it in a single layer in the air fryer basket. Cook in batches, if necessary, to avoid overcrowding the fryer.
- Cook for 5 minutes, turn bread pieces and cook for an additional 5 minutes.

Nutrition Facts

- Calories: 232; Protein 11.2g; Carbohydrates 28.6g; Fat 7.4g; Cholesterol 188.4mg; Sodium 423.4mg.

32. AIR FRYER FISH STICKS

Prep Time: 10 mins

Cook Time: 10 mins

Total Time: 20 mins

Ingredient

- 1 pound cod fillets
- ¼ cup all-purpose flour
- 1 egg
- ½ cup panko bread crumbs
- ¼ cup grated parmesan cheese
- 1 tablespoon parsley flakes
- 1 teaspoon paprika
- ½ teaspoon black pepper
- Cooking spray

Instructions

- Preheat an air fryer to 400 degrees F (200 degrees C).
- Pat fish dry with paper towels and cut into 1x3-inch sticks.
- Place flour in a shallow dish. Beat egg in a separate shallow dish. Combine panko, Parmesan cheese, parsley, paprika, and pepper in a third shallow dish.
- Coat each fish stick in flour, then dip in beaten egg, and finally coat in seasoned panko mixture.
- Spray the basket of the air fryer with nonstick cooking spray. Arrange 1/2 the sticks in the basket, making sure none are touching. Spray the top of each stick with cooking spray.
- Cook in the preheated air fryer for 5 minutes. Flip fish sticks and cook for an additional 5 minutes. Repeat with remaining fish sticks.

Nutrition Facts

- Calories: 200; Protein 26.3g; Carbohydrates 16.5g; Fat 4.1g; Cholesterol 92.5mg; Sodium 245mg.

33. AIR FRYER KETO CHICKEN WINGS

Prep Time: 5 mins

Cook Time: 15 mins

Total Time: 20 mins

Ingredient

- 3 pounds chicken wings
- 1 tablespoon taco seasoning mix
- 2 teaspoons olive oil

Instructions

- Combine chicken wings, taco seasoning, and oil in a resealable plastic bag. Shake to coat.
- Preheat the air fryer to 350 degrees F (175 degrees C) for 2 minutes.
- Place wings in the air fryer and cook for 12 minutes, turning after 6 minutes. Serve immediately.

Nutrition Facts

- Calories: 220; Protein 18.3g; Carbohydrates 1.2g; Fat 15.1g; Cholesterol 57.1mg; Sodium 187mg.

34. AIR-FRIED MEATLOAF

Prep Time: 10 mins

Cook Time: 45 mins

Additional Time: 1 day

Total Time: 1 day

Ingredient

- ½ pound ground pork
- ½ pound ground veal
- 1 large egg
- ¼ cup chopped fresh cilantro
- ¼ cup gluten-free bread crumbs
- 2 medium spring onions, diced
- ½ teaspoon ground black pepper
- ½ teaspoon Sriracha salt
- ½ cup ketchup
- 2 teaspoons gluten-free chipotle chili sauce
- 1 teaspoon olive oil
- 1 teaspoon blackstrap molasses

Instructions

- Preheat the air fryer to 400 degrees F (200 degrees C).
- Combine pork and veal in a nonstick baking dish that fits inside the air fryer basket. Make a well and add egg, cilantro, bread crumbs, spring onions, black pepper, and 1/2 teaspoon of Sriracha salt. Mix well using your hands. Form a loaf inside the baking dish.
- Combine ketchup, chipotle chili sauce, olive oil, and molasses in a small bowl and whisk well. Set aside, but do not refrigerate.
- Cook meatloaf in the air fryer for 25 minutes without opening the basket. Remove meatloaf and top with ketchup mixture, covering the top completely. Return meatloaf to air fryer and bake until internal temperature reaches 160 degrees F (71 degrees C), about 7 minutes more.
- Turn off the air fryer and let the meatloaf rest inside for 5 minutes. Take the meatloaf out and let rest 5 minutes more before slicing and serving.

Nutrition Facts

- Calories: 272; Protein 22.1g; Carbohydrates 13.3g; Fat 14.4g; Cholesterol 123.5mg; Sodium 536.1mg.

35. AIR-FRIED CRUMBED FISH

Prep Time: 10 mins

Cook Time: 12 mins

Total Time: 22 mins

Ingredient

- 1 cup dry bread crumbs
- ¼ cup vegetable oil
- 4 flounder fillets
- 1 egg, beaten
- 1 lemon, sliced

Instructions

- Preheat an air fryer to 350 degrees F (180 degrees C).
- Mix bread crumbs and oil in a bowl. Stir until

the mixture becomes loose and crumbly.
- Dip fish fillets into the egg; shake off any excess. Dip fillets into the bread crumb mixture; coat evenly and fully.
- Lay coated fillets gently in the preheated air fryer. Cook until fish flakes easily with a fork, about 12 minutes. Garnish with lemon slices.

Nutrition Facts
- Calories: 354; Protein 26.9g; Carbohydrates 22.5g; Fat 17.7g; Cholesterol 106.7mg; Sodium 308.9mg

36. AIR FRYER RANCH PORK CHOPS

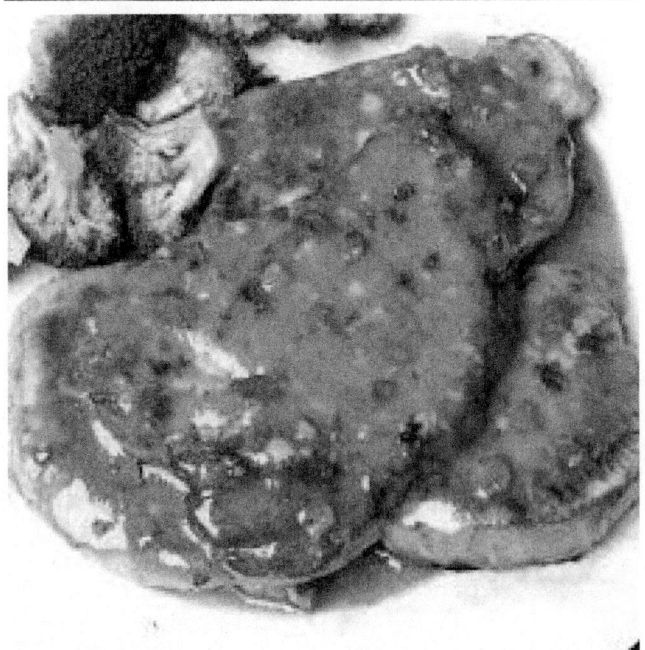

Prep Time: 5 mins

Cook Time: 10 mins

Additional Time: 10 mins

Total Time: 25 mins

Ingredient
- 4 boneless, center-cut pork chops, 1-inch thick
- cooking spray
- 2 teaspoons dry ranch salad dressing mix
- Aluminum foil

Instructions
- Place pork chops on a plate and lightly spray both sides with cooking spray. Sprinkle both sides with ranch seasoning mix and let sit at room temperature for 10 minutes.
- Spray the basket of an air fryer with cooking spray and preheat the air fryer to 390 degrees F (200 degrees C).
- Place chops in the preheated air fryer, working in batches if necessary, to ensure the fryer is not overcrowded.
- Cook for 5 minutes. Flip chops and cook 5 minutes more. Let rest on a foil-covered plate for 5 minutes before serving.

Nutrition Facts
- Calories: 260; Protein 40.8g; Carbohydrates 0.6g; Fat 9.1g; Cholesterol 106.6mg; Sodium 148.2mg.

37. AIR FRYER RIB-EYE STEAK

Prep Time: 5 mins

Cook Time: 15 mins

Additional Time: 2 hrs 5 mins

Total Time: 2 hrs 25 mins

Ingredient
- 2 rib-eye steaks, cut 1 1/2- inch thick
- 4 teaspoons grill seasoning (such as Montreal Steak Seasoning®)
- ¼ cup olive oil
- ½ cup reduced-sodium soy sauce

Instructions
- Combine steaks, soy sauce, olive oil, and seasoning in a large resealable bag. Marinate meat for at least 2 hours.
- Remove steaks from bag and discard the marinade. Pat excess oil off the steaks.
- Add about 1 tablespoon water to the bottom of the air fryer pan to prevent it from smoking during the cooking process.
- Preheat the air fryer to 400 degrees F (200 degrees C).
- Add steaks to air fryer and cook for 7 minutes. Turn steaks and cook for another 7 minutes until steak is medium-rare. For a medium steak, increase the total cook time to 16 minutes, flipping steak after 8 minutes.
- Remove steaks, keep warm, and let sit for about 4 minutes before serving.

Nutrition Facts

- Calories: 652; Protein 44g; Carbohydrates 7.5g; Fat 49.1g; Cholesterol 164.8mg; Sodium 4043.7mg.

38. AIR-FRIED SESAME-CRUSTED COD WITH SNAP PEAS

Prep Time: 10 mins Cook Time: 20 mins Total Time: 30 mins

Ingredient

- 4 (5 ounces) cod fillets
- salt and ground black pepper to taste
- 3 tablespoons butter, melted
- 2 tablespoons sesame seeds
- Vegetable oil
- 2 (6 ounce) packages sugar snap peas
- 3 cloves garlic, thinly sliced
- 1 medium orange, cut into wedges

Instructions

- Brush the air fryer basket with vegetable oil and preheat to 400 degrees F (200 degrees C).
- Thaw fish if frozen; blot dry with paper towels, and sprinkle lightly with salt and pepper.
- Stir together butter and sesame seeds in a small bowl. Set aside 2 tablespoons of the butter mixture for the fish. Toss peas and garlic with the remaining butter mixture and place in the air fryer basket.
- Cook peas in the preheated air fryer in batches, if needed, until just tender, tossing once, about 10 minutes. Remove and keep warm while cooking fish.
- Brush fish with 1/2 of the remaining butter mixture. Place fillets in an air fryer basket. Cook 4 minutes; turn fish. Brush with the remaining butter mixture. Cook 5 to 6 minutes more or until fish begins to flake when tested with a fork. Serve with snap peas and orange wedges.

Nutrition Facts

- Calories: 364; Protein 31.4g; Carbohydrates 22.9g; Fat 15.2g; Cholesterol 74.8mg; Sodium 201.5mg.

39. AIR FRYER MEATBALLS

Prep Time: 10 mins

Cook Time: 20 mins

Servings: 16

Ingredient

- 16 ounces lean ground beef
- 4 ounces ground pork
- 1 teaspoon Italian seasoning
- ½ teaspoon salt
- 2 cloves garlic, minced
- 1 egg
- ½ cup grated Parmesan cheese
- ⅓ cup Italian seasoned bread crumbs

Instructions

- Preheat the air fryer to 350 degrees F (175 degrees C).
- Combine beef, pork, Italian seasoning, salt, garlic, egg, Parmesan cheese, and bread crumbs

in a large bowl. Mix well until evenly combined. Form into 16 equally-sized meatballs using an ice cream scoop and place on a baking sheet.
- Place 1/2 of the meatballs in the basket of the air fryer and cook for 8 minutes. Shake the basket and cook 2 minutes more. Transfer to a serving plate and let rest for 5 minutes. Repeat with remaining meatballs.

Nutrition Facts
- Calories: 96; Protein 7.9g; Carbohydrates 2g; Fat 6.1g; Cholesterol 35.5mg; Sodium 170.4mg.

40. AIR FRYER HOT DOGS

Prep Time: 5 mins

Cook Time: 5 mins

Total Time: 10 mins

Servings: 4

Ingredient
- 4 hot dog buns
- 4 hot dogs

Instructions
- Preheat air fryer to 390 degrees F (200 degrees C).
- Place buns in the basket of the air fryer and cook for 2 minutes. Remove buns to a plate.
- Place hot dogs in the basket of the air fryer and cook for 3 minutes. Transfer hot dogs to buns.

41. AIR FRYER BAKED POTATOES

Prep Time: 5 mins

Cook Time: 1 hr

Total Time: 1 hr 5 mins

Servings: 2

Ingredient
- 2 large russet potatoes, scrubbed
- 1 tablespoon peanut oil
- ½ teaspoon coarse sea salt

Instructions
- Preheat air fryer to 400 degrees F (200 degrees C).
- Brush potatoes with peanut oil and sprinkle with salt. Place them in the air fryer basket and place the basket in the air fryer.
- Cook potatoes until done, about 1 hour. Test for doneness by piercing them with a fork.

Nutrition Facts
- Calories: 344; Protein 7.5g; Carbohydrates 64.5g; Fat 7.1g; Sodium 462.1mg.

42. CRUMBED CHICKEN TENDERLOINS (AIR FRIED)

Prep: 15 mins

Cook: 12 mins

Total: 27 mins

Servings: 4

Ingredient

- 1 egg
- ½ cup dry bread crumbs
- 2 tablespoons vegetable oil
- 8 chicken tenderloins

Instructions

- Preheat an air fryer to 350 degrees F (175 degrees C).
- Whisk egg in a small bowl.
- Mix bread crumbs and oil in a second bowl until the mixture becomes loose and crumbly.
- Dip each chicken tenderloin into the bowl of an egg; shake off any residual egg. Dip chicken into the crumb mixture, making sure it is evenly and fully covered. Lay chicken tenderloins into the basket of the air fryer. Cook until no longer pink in the center, about 12 minutes. An instant-read thermometer inserted into the center should read at least 165 degrees F (74 degrees C).

Nutrition Facts

- Calories: 253; Protein 26.2g; Carbohydrates 9.8g; Fat 11.4g; Cholesterol 109mg; Sodium 170.7mg.

43. AIR FRYER POTSTICKERS

Prep Time: 10 mins

Cook Time: 25 mins

Total Time: 35 mins

Servings: 24

Ingredient

- ½ pound ground pork
- 1 (4 ounces) can water chestnuts, drained and chopped
- 1 (4 ounces) can shiitake mushrooms, drained and chopped
- 2 tablespoons soy sauce
- 2 tablespoons sesame oil
- 1 tablespoon Sriracha sauce
- 1 (12 ounces) package round dumpling wrappers

Instructions

- Preheat an air fryer to 400 degrees F (200 degrees C).
- Combine ground pork, water chestnuts, shiitake mushrooms, sesame oil, soy sauce, and Sriracha in a large skillet over medium-high heat. Cook until pork is no longer pink, about 6 minutes. Remove from heat and let sit until cool enough to handle.
- Layout 8 dumpling wrappers on a clean work surface. Place a heaping teaspoonful of pork mixture in the middle of each wrapper. Pull both sides up like a taco and pinch the tops until sealed.
- Cook in batches in the preheated air fryer for 3 minutes. Use tongs to flip the potstickers and

cook 3 minutes more. Transfer to a paper-towel-lined plate. Repeat with remaining dumpling wrappers and filling.

Nutrition Facts

- Calories: 70; Protein 2.7g; Carbohydrates 8.7g; Fat 2.6g; Cholesterol 4.7mg; Sodium 273.1mg.

44. HAM AND MOZZARELLA EGGPLANT BOATS

Prep Time: 17 minutes

Ingredients

- 1 eggplant
- 4 ham slices, chopped
- 1 cup shredded mozzarella cheese, divided
- 1 tsp. dried parsley
- Salt and pepper, to taste

Instructions

- Preheat the air fryer to 330 degrees.
- Peel the eggplant and cut it lengthwise in half. Scoop some of the flash out.Season with salt and pepper.
- Divide half the mozzarella cheese between the eggplants.
- Place the ham on top of the mozzarella.
- Top with the remaining mozzarella cheese.
- Sprinkle with parsley.Cook 12 minutes

Nutrition Facts

Calories 323.1, Carbohydrates 15.7 g, Fat 16.4 g, Protein 28.3 g

45. LEFTOVER TURKEY AND MUSHROOM SANDWICH

Prep Time: 15 MInutes

Ingredients

- 1/3 cup shredded leftover turkey
- 1/3 cup sliced mushrooms
- 1 tbsp. butter, divided
- 2 tomato slices
- ½ tsp. red pepper flakes
- ¼ tsp. salt
- ¼ tsp. black pepper
- 1 hamburger bun

Instructions

- Preheat the air fryer to 350 degrees F.
- Melt half of the butter and add the mushrooms.
- Cook for about 4 minutes.
- Meanwhile, cut the bun in half and spread the remaining butter on the outside of the bun.
- Place the turkey on one half of the bun.Arrange the mushroom slices on top of the turkey.Place the tomato slices on top of the mushrooms.
- Sprinkle with salt pepper and red pepper flakes.Top with the other bun half.Cook for 5 minutes.

Nutrition Facts

Calories 318.3, Carbohydrates 25.6 g, Fat 16.4 g, Protein 18.4 g

46. ITALIAN SAUSAGE PATTIES

Prep Time: 20 Minutes

Ingredients

- 1 lb. ground Italian sausage
- ¼ cup breadcrumbs
- 1 tsp. dried parsley
- 1 tsp. red pepper Flakes
- ½ tsp. salt
- ¼ tsp. black peppe
- r¼ tsp. garlic powder
- 1 egg, beaten

Instructions

- Preheat the air fryer to 350 degrees F.
- Combine all of the **Ingredients** in a large bowl.Line a baking sheet with parchment paper.
- Make patties out of the sausage mixture and arrange them on the baking sheet.Cook for about 15 minutes.
- Serve as desired (they are amazing with tzatziki sauce)

Nutrition Facts

Calories 332.3 Carbohydrates 6.2 g, Fat 24.6 g, Protein 18.6 g

47. AIR-FRIED POPCORN CHICKEN GIZZARDS

Prep Time: 10 mins Cook Time: 45 mins Additional Time: 5 mins Total Time: 1 hr

Ingredient

- 1 pound chicken gizzards
- ⅓ cup all-purpose flour
- 1 ½ teaspoon seasoned salt
- ½ teaspoon ground black pepper
- ½ teaspoon garlic powder
- ½ teaspoon paprika
- 1 pinch cayenne pepper (optional)
- 1 large egg, beaten
- Cooking spray

Instructions

- Bring a large pot of water to a boil. Cut gizzards into bite-sized pieces and add to the boiling water. Boil for 30 minutes. Drain.
- Combine flour, seasoned salt, pepper, garlic powder, paprika, and cayenne in a flat plastic container. Snap the lid on and shake until combined.
- Add gizzards to the seasoned flour. Snap the lid back on and shake until evenly coated.
- Place beaten egg in a separate bowl. Dip each gizzard piece into the beaten egg and then place it back in the seasoned flour. Snap the lid on and shake one last time. Let sit for 5 minutes while the air fryer preheats.
- Preheat the air fryer to 400 degrees F (200 degrees C).
- Place gizzards in the basket and spray the tops with cooking spray. Cook for 4 minutes. Shake the basket and spray any chalky spots with more cooking spray. Cook for 4 minutes more.

Nutrition Facts

- Calories: 237; Protein 23.6g; Carbohydrates 11.8g; Fat 10g; Cholesterol 330.8mg; Sodium 434.2mg

48. AIR FRYER CRAB RANGOON

Prep Time: 15 mins Cook Time: 20 mins Total Time: 35 mins

Ingredient

- 1 (8 ounces) package cream cheese, softened
- 4 ounces lump crab meat
- 2 tablespoons chopped scallions
- 1 teaspoon soy sauce
- 1 teaspoon Worcestershire sauce
- 1 serving nonstick cooking spray
- 24 each wonton wrappers
- 2 tablespoons Asian sweet chili sauce, for dipping

Instructions

- Combine cream cheese, crab meat, scallions, soy sauce, and Worcestershire sauce in a bowl; stir until evenly combined.
- Preheat an air fryer to 350 degrees F (175 degrees C). Spray the basket of the air fryer with cooking spray. Fill a small bowl with warm water.
- Place 12 wonton wrappers on a clean work surface. Spoon 1 teaspoon of cream cheese mixture into the center of each wonton wrapper. Dip index finger into the warm water and wet around the sides of each wonton wrapper. Crimp wrapper corners upwards to meet in the center to form dumplings.
- Place dumplings in the prepared basket and spray the tops with cooking spray.
- Cook dumplings until desired crispness, about 8 to 10 minutes. Transfer to a paper towel-lined plate.
- While the first batch is cooking, assemble the remaining dumplings with the remaining wrappers and filling.
- Serve with sweet chili sauce for dipping.

Nutrition Facts

- Calories: 127; Protein 5.1g; Carbohydrates 11.1g; Fat 6.9g; Cholesterol 29.1mg; Sodium 240.4mg.

49. MEXICAN-STYLE AIR FRYER STUFFED CHICKEN BREASTS

Prep Time: 20 mins

Cook Time: 10 mins

Total Time: 30 mins

Servings: 2

Ingredients

- 4 extra-long toothpicks
- 4 teaspoons chili powder, divided
- 4 teaspoons ground cumin, divided
- 1 skinless, boneless chicken breast
- 2 teaspoons chipotle flakes
- 2 teaspoons mexican oregano
- Salt and ground black pepper to taste
- ½ red bell pepper, sliced into thin strips
- ½ onion, sliced into thin strips
- 1 fresh jalapeno pepper, sliced into thin strips
- 2 teaspoons corn oil
- ½ lime, juiced

Instructions

- Place toothpicks in a small bowl and cover with water; let them soak to keep them from burning while cooking.
- Mix 2 teaspoons chili powder and 2 teaspoons cumin in a shallow dish.
- Preheat an air fryer to 400 degrees F (200 degrees C).
- Place chicken breast on a flat work surface. Slice horizontally through the middle. Pound each half using a kitchen mallet or rolling pin until

about 1/4-inch thick.
- Sprinkle each breast half equally with remaining chili powder, remaining cumin, chipotle flakes, oregano, salt, and pepper. Place 1/2 the bell pepper, onion, and jalapeno in the center of 1 breast half. Roll the chicken from the tapered end upward and use 2 toothpicks to secure it. Repeat with other breast, spices, and vegetables and secure with remaining toothpicks. Roll each roll-up in the chili-cumin mixture in the shallow dish while drizzling with olive oil until evenly covered.
- Place roll-ups in the air-fryer basket with the toothpick side facing up. Set timer for 6 minutes.
- Turn roll-ups over. Continue cooking in the air fryer until juices run clear and an instant-read thermometer inserted into the center reads at least 165 degrees F (74 degrees C), about 5 minutes more.
- Drizzle lime juice evenly on roll-ups before serving.

Nutrition Facts
- Calories: 185; Protein 14.8g; Carbohydrates 15.2g; Fat 8.5g; Cholesterol 32.3mg; Sodium 170.8mg.

50. AIR FRYER CHIMICHANGAS

Prep Time: 15 mins

Cook Time: 20 mins

Total Time: 35 mins

Servings: 6

Ingredient
- 1 tablespoon vegetable oil
- ½ cup diced onion
- 2 cups shredded cooked chicken
- ½ (8 ounces) package Neufchatel cheese, softened
- 1 (4 ounces) can hot fire-roasted diced green chiles (such as Ortega®)
- ¼ cup chicken broth
- 1 ½ tablespoons chicken taco seasoning mix (such as McCormick®)
- ½ teaspoon salt
- ¼ teaspoon ground black pepper
- 6 (10 inches) flour tortillas
- 1 cup shredded Mexican cheese blend, or to taste
- Avocado oil cooking spray

Instructions
- Heat oil in a medium skillet. Add onion and cook until soft and translucent, 4 to 6 minutes. Add chicken, Neufchatel cheese, diced chiles, chicken broth, taco seasoning, salt, and pepper. Cook and stir until mixture is well combined and Neufchatel has softened been incorporated.
- Heat tortillas in a large skillet or directly on the grates of a gas stove until soft and pliable. Place 1/3 cup chicken mixture down the center of each tortilla and top with a heaping tablespoon of Mexican cheese. Fold top and bottom of tortillas over the filling, then roll each into a burrito shape. Mist with cooking spray and place in the basket of an air fryer.
- Air fry at 400 degrees F (200 degrees C) for 4 to 6 minutes. Flip each chimichanga over, mist with cooking spray, and air fry until lightly browned, 2 to 4 minutes more.

Nutrition Facts
- Calories: 455; Protein 24.8g; Carbohydrates 41g; Fat 20.6g; Cholesterol 69.8mg; Sodium 1291.5mg.

51. BREADED AIR FRYER PORK CHOPS

Prep Time: 10 mins

Cook Time: 10 mins

Total Time: 20 mins

Servings: 4

Ingredient

- 4 boneless, center-cut pork chops, 1-inch thick
- 1 teaspoon Cajun seasoning
- 1 ½ cups cheese and garlic-flavored croutons
- 2 eggs

Instructions

- Preheat the air fryer to 390 degrees F (200 degrees C).
- Place pork chops on a plate and season both sides with Cajun seasoning.
- Pulse croutons in a small food processor until they have a fine consistency; transfer to a shallow dish. Lightly beat eggs in a separate shallow dish. Dip pork chops into eggs, letting excess drip off. Coat chops in crouton breading and set on a plate. Mist chops with cooking spray.
- Spray basket of the air fryer with cooking spray and place chops inside, making sure to not overcrowd the fryer. You may have to do two batches depending on the size of your air fryer.
- Cook for 5 minutes. Flip chops and mist again with cooking spray if there are dry or powdery areas. Cook 5 minutes more. Repeat with remaining chops.

Nutrition Facts

- Calories: 394; Protein 44.7g; Carbohydrates 10g; Fat 18.1g; Cholesterol 218mg; Sodium 428.9mg.

52. AIR FRYER CRAB RANGOON

Prep Time: 15 mins

Cook Time: 20 mins

Total Time: 35 mins

Servings: 12

Ingredient

- 1 (8 ounces) package cream cheese, softened
- 4 ounces lump crab meat
- 2 tablespoons chopped scallions
- 1 teaspoon soy sauce
- 1 teaspoon Worcestershire sauce
- 1 serving nonstick cooking spray
- 24 each wonton wrappers
- 2 tablespoons Asian sweet chili sauce, for dipping

Instructions

- Combine cream cheese, crab meat, scallions, soy sauce, and Worcestershire sauce in a bowl; stir until evenly combined.
- Preheat an air fryer to 350 degrees F (175 degrees C). Spray the basket of the air fryer with cooking spray. Fill a small bowl with warm water.
- Place 12 wonton wrappers on a clean work surface. Spoon 1 teaspoon of cream cheese

mixture into the center of each wonton wrapper. Dip index finger into the warm water and wet around the sides of each wonton wrapper. Crimp wrapper corners upwards to meet in the center to form dumplings.
- Place dumplings in the prepared basket and spray the tops with cooking spray.
- Cook dumplings until desired crispness, about 8 to 10 minutes. Transfer to a paper towel-lined plate.
- While the first batch is cooking, assemble the remaining dumplings with the remaining wrappers and filling.
- Serve with sweet chili sauce for dipping.

Nutrition Facts

- Calories:234; Protein 5.1g; Carbohydrates 11.1g; Fat 6.9g; Cholesterol 29.1mg; Sodium 240.4mg.

53. LEMON-GARLIC AIR FRYER SALMON

Prep Time: 10 mins

Cook Time: 10 mins

Additional Time: 5 mins

Total Time: 25 mins

Ingredient

- 1 tablespoon melted butter
- ½ teaspoon minced garlic
- 2 (6 ounce) fillets center-cut salmon fillets with skin
- ¼ teaspoon lemon-pepper seasoning
- ⅛ teaspoon dried parsley
- Cooking spray
- 3 thin slices lemon, cut in half

Instructions

- Preheat the air fryer to 390 degrees F (200 degrees C).
- Combine melted butter and minced garlic in a small bowl.
- Rinse salmon fillets and dry with a paper towel. Brush with butter mixture and sprinkle with lemon-pepper seasoning and parsley.
- Spray the basket of the air fryer with cooking spray. Place salmon fillets in the basket, skin-side down, and top each with 3 lemon halves.
- Cook in the preheated air fryer for 8 to 10 minutes. Remove from the air fryer and let rest for 2 minutes before serving.

Nutrition Facts

- Calories: 293; Protein 33.6g; Carbohydrates 1.4g; Fat 16.4g; Cholesterol 108.3mg; Sodium 174.4mg.

54. AIR-FRIED CRUMBED FISH

Prep Time: 10 mins

Cook Time: 12 mins

Total Time: 22 mins

Ingredient

- 1 cup dry bread crumbs
- ¼ cup vegetable oil
- 4 flounder fillets
- 1 egg, beaten
- 1 lemon, sliced

Instructions

- Preheat an air fryer to 350 degrees F (180 degrees C).
- Mix bread crumbs and oil in a bowl. Stir until the mixture becomes loose and crumbly.
- Dip fish fillets into the egg; shake off any excess. Dip fillets into the bread crumb mixture; coat evenly and fully.
- Lay coated fillets gently in the preheated air fryer. Cook until fish flakes easily with a fork, about 12 minutes. Garnish with lemon slices.

Nutrition Facts

- Calories: 354; Protein 26.9g; Carbohydrates 22.5g; Fat 17.7g; Cholesterol 106.7mg; Sodium 308.9mg

55. LUNCH EGG ROLLS

Preparation time: 10 minutes Cooking time: 15 minutes

Ingredients:

- ½ cup mushrooms, chopped
- ½ cup carrots, grated
- ½ cup zucchini, grated
- 2 green onions, chopped
- 2 tablespoons soy sauce
- 8 egg roll wrappers
- 1 eggs, whisked
- 1 tablespoon cornstarch

Instructions:

- In a bowl, mix carrots with mushrooms, zucchini, green onions and soy sauce and stir well.
- Arrange egg roll wrappers on a working surface, divide veggie mix on each and roll well.
- In a bowl, mix cornstarch with egg, whisk well and brush eggs rolls with this mix.
- Seal edges, place all rolls in your preheated air fryer and cook them at 370 degrees F for 15 minutes.
- Arrange them on a platter and serve them for lunch.

Nutrition Facts:

calories 172, fat 6, fiber 6, carbs 8, protein 7

56. VEGGIE TOAST

Preparation time: 10 minutes Cooking time: 15 minutes

Ingredients:

- 1 red bell pepper, cut into thin strips
- 1 cup cremimi mushrooms, sliced
- 1 yellow squash, chopped
- 2 green onions, sliced
- 1 tablespoon olive oil
- 4 bread slices
- 2 tablespoons butter, soft
- ½ cup goat cheese, crumbled

Instructions:

- In a bowl, mix red bell pepper with mushrooms, squash, green onions and oil, toss, transfer to your air fryer, cook them at 350 degrees F for 10 minutes, shaking the fryer once and transfer them to a bowl.
- Spread butter on bread slices, place them in air fryer and cook them at 350 degrees F for 5 minutes.
- Divide veggie mix on each bread slice, top with crumbled cheese and serve for lunch.

Nutrition Facts:

calories 152, fat 3, fiber 4, carbs 7, protein 2

57. AIR FRYER RANCH PORK CHOPS

Prep Time: 5 mins

Cook Time: 10 mins

Additional Time: 10 mins

Total Time: 25 mins

Ingredient

- 4 boneless, center-cut pork chops, 1-inch thick
- cooking spray
- 2 teaspoons dry ranch salad dressing mix
- Aluminum foil

Instructions

- Place pork chops on a plate and lightly spray both sides with cooking spray. Sprinkle both sides with ranch seasoning mix and let sit at room temperature for 10 minutes.
- Spray the basket of an air fryer with cooking spray and preheat the air fryer to 390 degrees F (200 degrees C).
- Place chops in the preheated air fryer, working in batches if necessary, to ensure the fryer is not overcrowded.
- Cook for 5 minutes. Flip chops and cook 5 minutes more. Let rest on a foil-covered plate for 5 minutes before serving.

Nutrition Facts

- Calories: 260; Protein 40.8g; Carbohydrates 0.6g; Fat 9.1g; Cholesterol 106.6mg; Sodium 148.2mg.

58. FROZEN CHICKEN WINGS (NO THAW)

Cook Time 25 mins

Total Time 25 mins

Ingredients

- 1 pound frozen chicken wings Drums and flats
- Chicken rub to taste
- Salt and pepper to taste

Instructions

- Place the frozen wings in the air fryer basket.
- Air fry for 6 minutes on 400 degrees.
- Open the air fryer basket and use a wooden spoon or spatula to break apart the chicken. You may need to air fry it for a few additional minutes if 6 minutes isn't long enough for you.
- Air fry the wings for an additional 4 minutes on 400 degrees.
- Open the basket and season both sides of the wings.
- Air fry on 400 degrees for 8 minutes.
- Open the basket and flip the wings.
- Air fry for an additional 5 minutes on 400 degrees or until the wings have reached your desired level of crispiness, and an internal temperature of 165 degrees. The amount of wings you use and the air fryer brand and model you use may alter the cooking time. If you use more wings, allow a longer cooking time and check in on the wings to monitor doneness.

Nutrition Facts

- Calories: 254; Protein 26.9g; Carbohydrates 22.5g; Fat 17.7g;

59. RIB-EYE STEAK

Prep Time: 5 mins

Cook Time: 15 mins

Additional Time: 2 hrs 5 mins

Total Time: 2 hrs 25 mins

Ingredient

- 2 rib-eye steaks, cut 1 1/2- inch thick
- 4 teaspoons grill seasoning (such as Montreal Steak Seasoning®)
- ¼ cup olive oil
- ½ cup reduced-sodium soy sauce

Instructions

- Combine steaks, soy sauce, olive oil, and seasoning in a large resealable bag. Marinate meat for at least 2 hours.
- Remove steaks from bag and discard the

marinade. Pat excess oil off the steaks.
- Add about 1 tablespoon water to the bottom of the air fryer pan to prevent it from smoking during the cooking process.
- Preheat the air fryer to 400 degrees F (200 degrees C).
- Add steaks to air fryer and cook for 7 minutes. Turn steaks and cook for another 7 minutes until steak is medium-rare. For a medium steak, increase the total cook time to 16 minutes, flipping steak after 8 minutes.
- Remove steaks, keep warm, and let sit for about 4 minutes before serving.

Nutrition Facts
- Calories: 652; Protein 44g; Carbohydrates 7.5g; Fat 49.1g; Cholesterol 164.8mg; Sodium 4043.7mg.

60. AIR-FRIED SESAME-CRUSTED COD WITH SNAP PEAS

Prep Time: 10 mins

Cook Time: 20 mins

Total Time: 30 mins

Ingredient
- 4 (5 ounces) cod fillets
- salt and ground black pepper to taste
- 3 tablespoons butter, melted
- 2 tablespoons sesame seeds
- Vegetable oil
- 2 (6 ounce) packages sugar snap peas
- 3 cloves garlic, thinly sliced
- 1 medium orange, cut into wedges

Instructions
- Brush the air fryer basket with vegetable oil and preheat to 400 degrees F (200 degrees C).
- Thaw fish if frozen; blot dry with paper towels, and sprinkle lightly with salt and pepper.
- Stir together butter and sesame seeds in a small bowl. Set aside 2 tablespoons of the butter mixture for the fish. Toss peas and garlic with the remaining butter mixture and place in the air fryer basket.
- Cook peas in the preheated air fryer in batches, if needed, until just tender, tossing once, about 10 minutes. Remove and keep warm while cooking fish.
- Brush fish with 1/2 of the remaining butter mixture. Place fillets in an air fryer basket. Cook 4 minutes; turn fish. Brush with the remaining butter mixture. Cook 5 to 6 minutes more or until fish begins to flake when tested with a fork. Serve with snap peas and orange wedges.

Nutrition Facts
- Calories: 364; Protein 31.4g; Carbohydrates 22.9g; Fat 15.2g; Cholesterol 74.8mg; Sodium 201.5mg.

Air Fryer Seafoods Recipes

61. AIR FRYER COCONUT SHRIMP

Prep Time: 30 mins

Cook Time: 15 mins

Total Time: 45 mins

Ingredient
- ½ cup all-purpose flour
- 1 ½ teaspoon ground black pepper
- 2 large eggs
- ⅔ cup unsweetened flaked coconut
- ⅓ cup panko bread crumbs
- 12 ounces uncooked medium shrimp, peeled and deveined
- cooking spray
- ½ teaspoon kosher salt, divided
- ¼ cup honey
- ¼ cup lime juice

- 1 serrano chile, thinly sliced
- 2 teaspoons chopped fresh cilantro

Instructions

- Stir together flour and pepper in a shallow dish. Lightly beat eggs in a second shallow dish. Stir together coconut and panko in a third shallow dish. Hold each shrimp by the tail, dredge in flour mixture, and shake off excess. Then dip floured shrimp in egg, and allow any excess to drip off. Finally, dredge in coconut mixture, pressing to adhere. Place on a plate. Coat shrimp well with cooking spray.
- Preheat air fryer to 400 degrees F (200 degrees C). Place 1/2 the shrimp in the air fryer and cook for about 3 minutes. Turn shrimp over and continue cooking until golden, about 3 minutes more. Season with 1/4 teaspoon salt. Repeat with remaining shrimp.
- Meanwhile, whisk together honey, lime juice, and serrano chile in a small bowl for the dip.
- Sprinkle fried shrimp with cilantro and serve with dip.

Nutrition Facts

- Calories: 236; Protein 13.8g; Carbohydrates 27.6g; Fat 9.1g; Cholesterol 147.1mg; Sodium 316.4mg

62. PECAN CRUSTED SALMON

Preparation time: 20mins

Ingredients

- ½ cup pecans
- 3 tbsp. fresh chopped parsley
- 1 tsp. salt
- ½ tsp. ground black pepper
- 3 tbsp. Dijon mustard
- 3 tbsp. olive oil
- 1 tbsp. honey
- ½ cup Panko breadcrumbs
- 4 salmon filets 1 tbsp. lemon juice

Instructions

- Preheat air fryer to 390 degrees F.
- In a small bowl combine the mustard, oil, and honey. Combine the Panko, pecans, parsley, salt, and pepper in a food processor and process until crumbs are fine.
- Dip the salmon in the mustard mixture then dip the salmon into the pecan mixture, pressing the pecans into all sides of the fish.
- Place the coated salmon in the fryer basket and cook for 10 minutes.
- Drizzle with lemon juice.

Nutrition facts:

Calorie 353.2 Fats 24.8g Fiber 1.1g Carbs 1.7g Protein 30.5g

63. BROILED TILAPIA DONE

Preparation time: 9mins

Ingredients

- 1 to 1 1/2 lb. tilapia fillets
- molly mcbutter or butter buds
- light spritz of canola oil from an oil spritzer
- Old Bay seasoning,
- lemon pepper
- salt

Instructions

- Thaw fillets, if frozen. Spray the basket of your air fryer with cooking spray.
- Place fillets in the basket (do not stack them) and season to taste with the spices. Spray lightly with oil.
- Set temperature at 400 degrees and set timer for 7 minutes.
- When the timer goes off, check for doneness. Fish should flake easily with a fork.
- Serve and enjoy with your favorite veggies.

Nutrition facts:

Calorie 110 Fats 3g Fiber 0g Carbs 23g

64. PRAWN CURRY

Preparation time: 15mins

Ingredients

- 2 tbsp. curry powder
- 1 medium finely chopped onion
- 1½ cup chicken broth
- ½ tsp. of coriander
- 6 king prawns
- 1 tsp. salt
- ½ tsp. ground black pepper
- 1 tbsp. olive oil
- 1 tbsp. tomato paste

Instructions

Preheat the air fryer to 370 degrees F. Season the prawns with salt and pepper.

Cook for 7 minutes. Meanwhile, heat the olive oil in a large skillet. Once hot add the onion.

Cook until soft. Sit in the curry, tomato paste, and coriander.

Cook, stirring, for 1 minute.

Add the chicken broth and stir until smooth.

Remove prawns from the fryer and add to the sauce.

Nutrition facts:

Calorie 294.2 Fats 11g Fiber 7.4g Carbs 21.4g

65. CRUSTED HALIBUT

Preparation time: 30mins

Ingredients

- 2 tsp. lemon zest
- 1 tsp. salt
- ½ tsp. ground black pepper
- ¾ cup Panko bread crumbs
- ½ cup fresh parsley, chopped
- ¼ cup fresh dill, chopped
- 4 halibut filets
- 1 tbsp. olive oil

Instructions

- Preheat the air fryer to 390 degrees F.
- Combine all **Ingredients** except halibut and olive oil in a food processor and pulse until the mixture is a fine crumb.
- gently coat the halibut in the mixture and place inside the fryer basket.
- Drizzle with olive oil and cook for 25 minutes.

Nutrition facts:

Calorie 454

Fats 15g

Fiber 5g

Carbs 38g

Protein 4g

66. SHRIMP AND MUSHROOM RISOTTO

Preparation time: 30mins

Ingredients

- 4 Chicken Legs
- 2 tbsp. Olive Oil
- 4 tsp. dried Basil
- 2 tsp. minced garlic
- Pinch of Pepper
- Pinch of Salt
- 1 Lemon, sliced

Instructions

- Preheat your Air Fryer to 350 degrees F.
- Brush the chicken with the oil and sprinkle with the remaining **Ingredients**.
- Place in the Air Fryer and arrange the lemon slices around the chicken legs.
- Close the lid and cook for 20 minutes.

Nutrition facts:

Calorie 328.3 Fats 14.5g Fiber 2.3g Carbs 24.1g Protein 24.4g

67. HALIBUT SITKA

Preparation time: 20mins

Ingredients

- ½ cup green onion, chopped
- ½ cup mayonnaise
- ½ cup sour cream
- 6 (8 oz.) skinless halibut filets
- 1 tsp. salt
- ½ tsp. ground black pepper
- 1 tsp. dry dill

Instructions

- Preheat the air fryer to 390 degrees F
- Season the halibut with salt and pepper, place on the fryer plate.
- In a small bowl, combine the remaining **Ingredients**.
- Mix well then spread over the top of the halibut. Cook for 15 minutes.

Nutrition facts:

Calorie 333.26 Fats 37.03g Fiber 0.06g Carbs 1.74g Protein 22.17g

68. AIR FRIED CALAMARI AND TOMATO PASTA

Preparation time: 25mins

Ingredients

- 2 cloves garlic, minced
- 1 lb. sliced calamari, cut into rings
- 1 egg 1 cup Italian bread crumbs
- 1 tbsp. of olive oil
- ½ cup diced onion
- 2 tsps. Italian seasoning

- 2 (15 oz.) cans diced tomatoes, drained
- 1 lb. dry angel hair pasta
- ½ cup grated parmesan

Instructions

- Preheat fryer to 360 degrees.
- Dip the calamari into the egg and then into the breadcrumbs. Coating all sides. Place in the air fryer basket and drizzle with olive oil. Cook for 15 minutes. Meanwhile, bring a large pot of water to a boil.
- Add the pasta and cook for 10 minutes or until tender. Drain. Combine the pasta, garlic, onion, Italian seasoning, and diced tomatoes. Heat just until hot. Spoon on to a serving plate. Remove calamari from air fryer and place on top of pasta. Sprinkle with Parmesan

Nutrition facts:

Calorie 303.6 Fats 14.2g Fiber 0.06g Carbs 28.3g Protein 18.7g

69. AIR FRYER COCONUT SHRIMP

Prep Time: 30 mins

Cook Time: 15 mins

Total Time: 45 mins

Ingredient

- ½ cup all-purpose flour
- 1 ½ teaspoon ground black pepper
- 2 large eggs
- ⅔ cup unsweetened flaked coconut
- ⅓ cup panko bread crumbs
- 12 ounces uncooked medium shrimp, peeled and deveined
- cooking spray
- ½ teaspoon kosher salt, divided
- ¼ cup honey
- ¼ cup lime juice
- 1 serrano chile, thinly sliced
- 2 teaspoons chopped fresh cilantro

Instructions

- Stir together flour and pepper in a shallow dish. Lightly beat eggs in a second shallow dish. Stir together coconut and panko in a third shallow dish. Hold each shrimp by the tail, dredge in flour mixture, and shake off excess. Then dip floured shrimp in egg, and allow any excess to drip off. Finally, dredge in coconut mixture, pressing to adhere. Place on a plate. Coat shrimp well with cooking spray.
- Preheat air fryer to 400 degrees F (200 degrees C). Place 1/2 the shrimp in the air fryer and cook for about 3 minutes. Turn shrimp over and continue cooking until golden, about 3 minutes more. Season with 1/4 teaspoon salt. Repeat with remaining shrimp.
- Meanwhile, whisk together honey, lime juice, and serrano chile in a small bowl for the dip.
- Sprinkle fried shrimp with cilantro and serve with dip.

Nutrition Facts

Calories: 236; Protein 13.8g; Carbohydrates 27.6g; Fat 9.1g; Cholesterol 147.1mg; Sodium 316.4mg.

70. AIR-FRIED SHRIMP

Prep Time: 5 mins

Cook Time: 10 mins

Total Time: 15 mins

Servings: 4

Ingredient

- 1 tablespoon butter, melted
- 1 teaspoon lemon juice
- ½ teaspoon garlic granules
- ⅛ teaspoon salt
- 1 pound large shrimp - peeled, deveined, and tails removed
- Perforated parchment paper

- ⅛ cup freshly grated parmesan cheese

Instructions

- Place melted butter in a medium bowl. Mix in lemon juice, garlic granules, and salt. Add shrimp and toss to coat.
- Line air fryer basket with perforated parchment paper. Place shrimp in the air fryer basket and sprinkle with Parmesan cheese.
- Cook shrimp in the air fryer at 400 degrees F (200 degrees C) until shrimp are bright pink on the outside and the meat is opaque for about 8 minutes.

Nutrition Facts

- Calories: 125; Protein 19.6g; Carbohydrates 0.5g; Fat 4.6g; Cholesterol 182.4mg; Sodium 329.7mg.

71. AIR-FRIED SHRIMP

Prep Time: 5 mins

Cook Time: 10 mins

Total Time: 15 mins

Servings: 4

Ingredient

- 1 tablespoon butter, melted
- 1 teaspoon lemon juice
- ½ teaspoon garlic granules
- ⅛ teaspoon salt
- 1 pound large shrimp - peeled, deveined, and tails removed
- Perforated parchment paper
- ⅛ cup freshly grated parmesan cheese

Instructions

- Place melted butter in a medium bowl. Mix in lemon juice, garlic granules, and salt. Add shrimp and toss to coat.
- Line air fryer basket with perforated parchment paper. Place shrimp in the air fryer basket and sprinkle with Parmesan cheese.
- Cook shrimp in the air fryer at 400 degrees F (200 degrees C) until shrimp are bright pink on the outside and the meat is opaque for about 8 minutes.

Nutrition Facts

- Calories: 125; Protein 19.6g; Carbohydrates 0.5g; Fat 4.6g; Cholesterol 182.4mg; Sodium 329.7mg.

72. GARLIC PARMESAN AIR FRIED SHRIMP RECIPE

Prep Time: 5 Minutes

Cook Time: 10 Minutes

Total Time: 15 Minutes

Ingredients

- 1lb shrimp, deveined and peeled (you can leave tails on if desired)
- 1 tbsp olive oil
- 1 tsp salt
- 1 tsp fresh cracked pepper
- 1 tbsp lemon juice
- 6 cloves garlic, diced
- 1/2 cup grated parmesan cheese
- 1/4 cup diced cilantro or parsley, to garnish (optional)

Instructions

- In a large bowl, add shrimp and coat in olive oil and lemon juice, season with salt and pepper, and garlic.
- Cover with plastic wrap and refrigerate for 1-3 hours. (Optional, for more lemon flavor.)
- Toss parmesan cheese into the bowl with shrimp, creating a "breading" for the shrimp.
- Preheat air fryer.
- Set air fryer to 350 for 10 minutes, add shrimp to the basket and cook.

- Shrimp is done when it is opaque white and pink.
- Serve immediately.

Nutrition Information

- Calories: 151 Total Fat: 6g Saturated Fat: 2g Trans Fat: 0g Unsaturated Fat: 3g Cholesterol: 167mg Sodium: 1256mg Carbohydrates: 4g Protein: 20g

73. PARMESAN TILAPIA

Prep Time: 15 minutes

Ingredients:

¾ cup grated Parmesan cheese

1 tbsp. olive oil

2 tsp. paprika

1 tbsp. chopped parsley

¼ tsp. garlic powder¼ tsp. salt4 tilapia fillets

Instructions:

Preheat the air fryer to 350 degrees F.Mix parsley, Parmesan, garlic, salt, and paprika in a shallow bowl.Brush the olive oil over the fillets, and then coat them with the Parmesan mixture.Place the tilapia onto a lined baking sheet, and then into the air fryer.Cook for about 4 to 5 minutes on all sides.

Nutrition Facts

Calories 228.4, Carbohydrates 1.3 g, Fat 11.1 g, Protein 31.9 g

74. CHEESY BACON WRAPPED SHRIMP

Preparation time: 20mins

Ingredients

- 16 extra-large raw shrimp, peeled, deveined, and butterflied
- 16 (1 in) cubes cheddar jack cheese
- 16 slices of bacon, cooked half way
- ¼ cup BBQ sauce

Instructions

- Preheat the air fryer to 350 degrees F.
- Stuff each shrimp with a cheese cube and wrap with a slice of bacon.
- Secure the bacon to the shrimp with a toothpick.
- Brush the wrapped shrimp with BBQ sauce and place in the air fryer.
- Cook for 6 minutes.
- Remove and brush with additional BBQ sauce.

Nutrition facts:

Calorie 110 Protein 11g

75. SALMON QUICHE

Preparation time: 60mins

Ingredients

- 2 cups salmon, skinless and cubed
- 1 tsp. salt
- ¼ tsp. ground black pepper
- 1 (9 in) premade pie crust
- 3 large eggs
- 1 tbsp. Dijon mustard
- ¼ cup green onion, chopped
- ½ cup shredded mozzarella cheese
- 4 tbsp. heavy cream

Instructions

- Preheat the air fryer to a temperature of 350 degrees F
- Then, Season the salmon with salt and pepper to your taste. Set aside. Place the pre-made pie crust into individual quiche pans and press into the sides of the pans.
- Trim off any overhanging crust. Trim the dough onto the edges of the pan you intend to use or just let it stick out.

- Place the cubed salmon into the crust and top with the green onion and mozzarella. In a mixing bowl, combine the heavy cream, eggs, and mustard.
- Carefully pour over the salmon, being careful not cause the mixture to overflow.
- Carefully slide the quiche into the fryer basket and cook for 20 minutes.
- Let rest for 10 minutes before serving.

Nutrition facts:

Calorie 287.2,Fats 13g,Fiber 0.4g,Carbs 11.4g,Protein 29.5g

76. AIR FRYER GARLIC SHRIMP WITH LEMON

Prep Time: 5 mins

Cook Time: 10 mins

Total Time: 15 mins

Ingredients

- 1 pound (454 g) raw shrimp, peeled deveined,
- Vegetable oil or spray, to coat shrimp
- 1/4 teaspoon (1.25 ml) garlic powder
- Salt, to taste
- Black pepper, to taste
- Lemon wedges
- Minced parsley and/or chili flakes (optional)

Instructions

- In a bowl, toss the shrimp with the oil or spray to coat. Add garlic powder, salt, and pepper, and toss to evenly coat the shrimp.
- Add shrimp to the air fryer basket in a single layer.
- Air Fry at 400°F for about 8-14 minutes, gently shaking and flipping the shrimp over halfway through cooking. Cooking times will vary depending on the size of shrimp and on different air fryer brands and styles.
- Transfer shrimp to the bowl, squeeze lemon juice on top. Sprinkle parsley and/or chili flakes and serve hot.

Nutrition Value

- Calories: 164kcal | Carbohydrates: 1g | Protein: 31g | Fat: 3g | Saturated Fat: 1g | Cholesterol: 381mg | Sodium: 1175mg | Potassium: 121mg | Sugar: 1g | Vitamin C: 6mg | Calcium: 219mg | Iron: 3mg

77. SHRIMP POKE

Active Time: 30 mins

Total Time: 30 mins

Servings: 4

Ingredient

- ¾ cup thinly sliced scallion greens
- ¼ cup reduced-sodium tamari
- 1 ½ tablespoons mirin
- 1 ½ tablespoon toasted (dark) sesame oil
- 1 tablespoon white sesame seeds
- 2 teaspoons grated fresh ginger
- ½ teaspoon crushed red pepper (Optional)
- 12 ounces cooked shrimp, cut into 1/2-inch pieces
- 2 cups cooked brown rice
- 2 tablespoons rice vinegar
- 2 cups sliced cherry tomatoes
- 2 cups diced avocado
- ¼ cup chopped cilantro
- ¼ cup toasted black sesame seeds

Instructions

- Whisk scallion greens, tamari, mirin, oil, white sesame seeds, ginger, and crushed red pepper, if using, in a medium bowl. Set aside 2 tablespoons of the sauce in a small bowl.
- Add shrimp to the sauce in the medium bowl and gently toss to coat.
- Combine rice and vinegar in a large bowl.
- Divide among 4 bowls and top each with 3/4 cup shrimp, 1/2 cup each tomato and avocado,

and 1 tablespoon each cilantro and black sesame seeds. Drizzle with the reserved sauce and serve.

Nutrition Facts

- Calories: 460; Protein 28.9g; Carbohydrates 40.2g; Dietary Fiber 9.9g; Sugars 4.5g; Fat 22.1g; Saturated Fat 3.2g;; Calcium 113.2mg; Iron 3.2mg; Magnesium 145.1mg; Potassium 939.3mg; Sodium 860.6mg.

Air Fryer Meat Recipes

78. PERFECT AIR FRYER STEAK: PALEO, WHOLE30, KETO, EASY!

Prep Time: 5 Mins

Cook Time: 12 Mins

Total Time: 17 Mins

Ingredients

- 2 sirloin steaks
- 2–3 tbsp steak seasoning
- Spray oil or cooking fat of choice (I prefer avocado oil)

Instructions

- First, pat the steak dry and let come to room temperature
- Spray (or brush) oil lightly on the steak and season liberally
- Spray or coat the bottom of the air fryer basket with oil and place the steaks into the air fryer. The steaks can be touching or sort of "smooshed" in the basket.
- Cook at 400 degrees F. for 6 minutes, flip the steaks, and cook for another 6 minutes. If you want your steak more well-done, add 2-3 minutes. Let rest before serving.

Nutritional Value

- Calories: 195kcal | Carbohydrates: 5g | Protein: 12g |Saturated Fat: 6g | Cholesterol:44mg | Sodium: 43mg | Potassium: 321mg | Fiber: 2g | Sugar: 1g | Calcium: 15mg | Iron: 3mg

79. HOW TO MAKE STEAK IN THE AIR FRYER

Prep Time: 5 Minutes

Cook Time: 15 Minutes

Total Time: 20 Minutes

Ingredients

- 2 Pounds Steak (I Used Delmonico)
- Salt
- Pepper
- Garlic Powder
- 2 Tbs Butter

Instructions

- Preheat your air fryer to 400 for about 5 minutes
- Salt and pepper both sides of the steak
- Place a pad of butter on top of each steak
- Place on the top rack of your air fryer
- Cook on-air fry for 15 minutes for medium-well
- Flip over after 7 minutes
- For Medium-rare cook for 10 minutes flipping after 5
- For well-done cook for 20 minutes flipping after 10 minutes
- Remove steak and let rest for 5 minutes and serve

Nutrition Information:

Calories: 1371| Total Fat: 95g| Saturated Fat: 40g| Trans Fat: 0g| Unsaturated Fat: 41g| Cholesterol: 471mg| Sodium: 619mg| Carbohydrates: 2g| Fiber: 0g| Sugar: 0g| Protein: 119g

80. AIR FRYER MEATBALLS (LOW CARB)

Prep Time: 10 minutes

Cook Time: 14 minutes

Total Time: 24 minutes

Servings: 3 -4

Ingredients

- 1 lb Lean Ground Beef
- 1/4 Cup Marinara Sauce
- 1 Tablespoon Dried Minced Onion or Freeze Dried Shallots
- 1 teaspoon Minced Garlic I used freeze-dried
- 1 teaspoon Pizza Seasoning or Italian Seasoning
- 1/3 Cup Shredded Parmesan
- 1 Egg
- Salt and Pepper to taste
- Shredded Mozzarella Cheese optional
- 1 1/4 cups Marinara Sauce optional

Instructions

- Mix together all ingredients except reserve 1 1/4 cup of the marinara sauce and the mozzarella cheese.
- Form mixture into 12 meatballs and place in a single layer in the air fryer basket.
- Cook in the air fryer at 350 for 11 minutes.
- Optional: Place meatballs in an air fryer pan, toss in remaining marinara sauce, and top with mozzarella cheese. Place air fryer pan into the basket and cook at 350 for 3 minutes.

Nutritional Value

- Calories: 572kcal | Carbohydrates: 1g | Protein: 46g | Fat: 43g | Saturated Fat: 22g | Cholesterol: 168mg | Sodium: 219mg | Potassium: 606mg | Sugar: 1g | Vitamin A: 355IU | Calcium: 16mg | Iron: 4mg

81. AIR FRYER ROAST BEEF

Prep Time: 5 mins

Cook Time: 35 mins

Total Time: 40 mins

Ingredients

- 2 lb beef roast top round or eye of round is best
- Oil for spraying
- Rub
- 1 tbs kosher salt
- 1 tsp black pepper
- 2 tsp garlic powder
- 1 tsp summer savory or thyme

Instructions

- Mix all rub ingredients and rub into the roast.
- Place fat side down in the basket of the air fryer (or set up for rotisserie if your air fryer is so equipped)
- Lightly spray with oil.
- Set fryer to 400 degrees F and air fry for 20 minutes; turn fat-side up and spray lightly with oil. Continue cooking for 15 additional minutes at 400 degrees F.
- Remove the roast from the fryer, tent with foil, and let the meat rest for 10 minutes.
- The time given should produce a rare roast which should be 125 degrees F on a meat thermometer. Additional time will be needed for medium, medium-well, and well. Always use a meat thermometer to test the temperature.
- Approximate times for medium and well respectively are 40 minutes and 45 minutes. Remember to always use a meat thermometer as times are approximate and fryers differ by wattage.

Nutrition

- Calories: 238kcal | Carbohydrates: 1g | Protein: 25g | Fat: 14g | Saturated Fat: 6g | Cholesterol: 89mg | Sodium: 1102mg | Potassium: 448mg | Vitamin A: 55IU | Vitamin C: 0.3mg | Calcium: 37mg | Iron: 3mg

82. AIR FRYER STUFFED PEPPERS

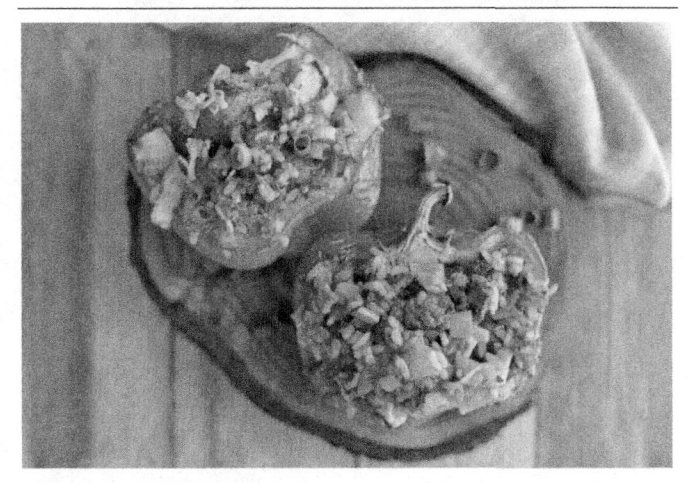

Prep Time: 15 Minutes

Cook Time: 15 Minutes

Ingredients

- 6 Green Bell Peppers
- 1 Lb Lean Ground Beef
- 1 Tbsp Olive Oil
- 1/4 Cup Green Onion Diced
- 1/4 Cup Fresh Parsley
- 1/2 Tsp Ground Sage
- 1/2 Tsp Garlic Salt
- 1 Cup Cooked Rice
- 1 Cup Marinara Sauce More to Taste
- 1/4 Cup Shredded Mozzarella Cheese

Instructions

- Warm-up a medium-sized skillet with the ground beef and cook until well done.
- Drain the beef and return to the pan.
- Add in the olive oil, green onion, parsley, sage, and salt. Mix this well.
- Add in the cooked rice and marinara, mix well.
- Cut the top off of each pepper and clean the seeds out.
- Scoop the mixture into each of the peppers and place it in the basket of the air fryer. (I did 4 the first round, 2 the second to make them fit.)
- Cook for 10 minutes at 355*, carefully open and add cheese.
- Cook for an additional 5 minutes or until peppers are slightly soft and cheese is melted.

Nutrition Information

- Total Fat: 13g| Saturated Fat: 4g| Trans Fat: 0g| Unsaturated Fat: 7g| Cholesterol: 70mg| Sodium: 419mg|

83. AIR FRYER STEAK

Prep Time: 10 mins

Cook Time: 15 mins

Resting Time: 8 mins

Total Time: 30 mins

Ingredients

- 2 (10 to 12 ounces EACH) sirloin steaks, about one inch thick, and at room temperature which is important for proper and even cooking.
- ½ tablespoon olive oil OR olive oil cooking spray, for the steaks
- 1 tablespoon kosher salt
- 1 tablespoon garlic powder
- 1 tablespoon onion powder
- ½ tablespoon paprika, sweet or smoked
- ½ tablespoon freshly ground black pepper
- 2 teaspoons dried herbs of choice

Instructions

- Preheat Air Fryer to 400°F.
- Rub both steaks with olive oil, or spray with cooking spray, and set aside.
- In a small mixing bowl combine salt, garlic powder, onion powder, paprika, pepper, and dried herbs. This makes enough seasoning for about 4 large steaks.
- Rub preferred amount of seasoning all over the steaks. Store leftover seasoning blends in a small airtight container and keeps it in a cool, dry place.
- Place 1 steak in the Air Fryer basket and cook for 6 minutes at 400°F.
- If you have a bigger Air Fryer, both steaks can fit in at the same time, but just make sure they aren't one on top of the other. You want a little space between the two.
- Flip over the steak and continue to cook for 4 to 5 more minutes, or until cooked through.
- Please use an Instant Read Thermometer to check for doneness; for a RARE steak, the temperature should register at 125°F to 130°F. For Medium-Rare, you want an internal temperature of 135°F.
- IF the steak isn't cooked through, it may be too thick and you'll want to return the steak to the air fryer and give it a minute or two to finish cooking.
- Repeat the cooking method with the other steak.
- Remove from air fryer and let rest for 5 to 8 minutes before cutting.
- Serve with a pat of butter and garnish with chopped parsley.

Nutrition Facts

- Fat: 17g
- Saturated Fat: 5g
- Cholesterol: 173mg
- Sodium: 3656mg
- Potassium: 1112mg
- Carbohydrates: 8g
- Fiber: 2g
- Sugar: 1g

84. AIR FRYER STEAK FAJITAS

Prep Time: 10 mins

Cook Time: 10 mins

Total Time: 20 mins

Ingredients

- 2 pounds flank steak strips
- 1 packet taco seasoning
- 1/2 red bell pepper, seeded, cored, and sliced
- 1/2 yellow bell pepper, seeded, cored, and sliced
- 1 onion, peeled and sliced
- 2 tablespoons freshly squeezed lime juice
- Cooking spray
- Flour tortillas
- Cilantro, chopped

Instructions

- Season steak with taco seasoning. Marinate for about 20 to 30 minutes.
- Preheat your air fryer to 400 degrees. Spray the air fryer tray with cooking spray,
- Arrange the seasoned beef on the air fryer tray, cooking in batches depending on the size of the air fryer.
- Add a layer of the sliced onions and a layer of bell peppers on top of the meat.
- Place in the air fryer for 10 minutes. Toss halfway through cooking to ensure the steak is cooked evenly.
- Remove from the air fryer and drizzle with lime juice.
- Serve in warm tortillas with fresh cilantro.

Nutrition

- Calories: 620kcal | Carbohydrates: 56g | Protein: 56g | Fat: 17g | Saturated Fat: 6g | Cholesterol: 136mg | Sodium: 1446mg | Potassium: 1014mg | Fiber: 5g | Sugar: 8g | Vitamin A: 1350IU | Vitamin C: 55mg | Calcium: 149mg | Iron: 7mg

85. AIR FRYER TACO CALZONES

Prep Time: 10 Minutes

Cook Time: 10 Minutes

Total Time: 20 Minutes

Ingredients

- 1 tube Pillsbury thin crust pizza dough
- 1 cup taco meat
- 1 cup shredded cheddar

Instructions

- Spread out your sheet of pizza dough on a clean surface. Using a pizza cutter, cut the dough into 4 even squares.
- Cut each square into a large circle using the pizza cutter. Set the dough scraps aside to make cinnamon sugar bites.
- Top one half of each circle of dough with 1/4 cup taco meat and 1/4 cup shredded cheese.
- Fold the empty half over the meat and cheese and press the edges of the dough together with a fork to seal it tightly. Repeat with all four calzones.
- Gently pick up each calzone and spray it with pan spray or olive oil. Arrange them in your Air Fryer basket.
- Cook the calzones at 325° for 8-10 minutes. Watch them closely at the 8-minute mark so you don't overcook them.
- Serve with salsa and sour cream.
- To make cinnamon sugar bites, cut the scraps of dough into even-sized pieces, about 2 inches long. Add them to the Air Fryer basket and cook at 325° for 5 minutes. Immediately toss with a 1:4 cinnamon-sugar mixture.

Nutrition Information

- Total Fat: 31g| Saturated Fat: 14g| Trans Fat: 1g| Unsaturated Fat: 14g| Cholesterol: 58mg| Sodium: 814mg| Carbohydrates: 38g| Fiber: 2g| Sugar: 1g| Protein: 18g

86. AIR FRYER STEAK BITES WITH MUSHROOMS

Prep Time: 10 mins

Cook Time: 15 mins

Total Time: 25 mins

Ingredients

- 2 lb beef
- 2 lb mushrooms
- 2 tbsp Worcester sauce
- 1 tbsp salt
- 1 tbsp pepper

Instructions

- Preheat an Air Fryer for 3 minutes at 400 °F. Cut beef into bite-size pieces and mushrooms into halves.
- Mushrooms and steak in a bowl
- Add Worchester sauce, salt, and pepper to the mixture. Let it sit for a few minutes.
- Steak and mushrooms withs seasoning
- Add beef and mushrooms to the air fryer basket. Air-dry it for 5 minutes.
- Uncooked steak and mushrooms in a basket
- Remove the basket and toss the steak bites to ensure all the sides are getting nice and crispy.
- Basket with steak and mushrooms
- Air fry for another 5-7 minutes. Once complete, check to make sure the temperature of the beef reached 145F.
- Steak bites with mushrooms in an air fryer basket

Nutrition Facts

- Fat: 31g Saturated Fat: 12g Cholesterol: 107mg Sodium: 1327mg Potassium: 948mg Carbohydrates: 7g Fiber: 2g Sugar: 4g Protein: 31g Vitamin C: 4mg Calcium: 42mg Iron: 4mg

87. AIR FRYER STEAK

Prep Time: 15min

Cook Time: 9min

Ingredients

- 2 boneless ribeye steaks
- 1 tablespoon steak rub
- 1 teaspoon kosher salt
- 1 tablespoon unsalted butter

Directions

- Rub steaks with steak rub and salt. Allow resting at room temperature for 15 to 30 minutes. The longer you allow them to rest with the rub on, the more flavorful they will be!
- Preheat air fryer for 5 minutes at 400°F (200°C).
- Arrange steaks in a single layer in an air fryer basket, work in batches as needed and cook about 9 minutes for medium-rare. The internal temperature should read at least 145°F (63°C).
- Transfer steak to a cutting board and put half the butter on each steak. Allow resting for at least 5 minutes before slicing into 1/2-inch thick slices.

Nutrition Facts

- Calories: 301; 23g Fat; 0.0g Carbohydrates; 23g

88. AIR FRYER ITALIAN-STYLE MEATBALLS

Active Time: 10 Mins

Total Time: 45 Mins

Yield: Serves 12 (2 meatballs)

Ingredients

- 2 tablespoons olive oil 1 medium shallot, minced (about 2 Tbsp.) 3 cloves garlic, minced (about 1 Tbsp.) 1/4 cup whole-wheat panko crumbs 2 tablespoons whole milk 2/3 pound lean ground beef 1/3 pound bulk turkey sausage 1 large egg, lightly beaten 1/4 cup finely chopped fresh flat-leaf parsley 1 tablespoon chopped fresh rosemary 1 tablespoon finely chopped fresh thyme 1 tablespoon Dijon mustard 1/2 teaspoon kosher salt

How To Make It

- Preheat air-fryer to 400°F. Heat oil in a medium nonstick pan over medium-high heat. Add shallot and cook until softened, 1 to 2 minutes. Add garlic and cook just until fragrant, 1 minute. Remove from heat.
- In a large bowl, combine panko and milk. Let stand 5 minutes.
- Add cooked shallot and garlic to the panko mixture, along with beef, turkey sausage egg, parsley, rosemary, thyme, mustard, and salt. Stir to gently combine.
- Gently shape mixture into 1 1/2-inch ball. Place shaped balls in a single-layer in the air-fryer basket. Cook half the meatballs at 400°F until lightly browned and cooked for 10 to 11 minutes. Remove and keep warm. Repeat with remaining meatballs.
- Serve warm meatballs with toothpicks as an appetizer or serve over pasta, rice, or spiralized zoodles for a main dish.

Nutritional Information

- Calories: 122| Fat: 8g| Sat fat: 2g| Unsatfat: 5g| Protein: 10g| Carbohydrate| 0g Fiber 0g| Sugars 0g| Added sugars: 0g| Sodium: 254mg

89. AIR FRYER STEAK

Prep Time: 5 mins, Cook Time: 25 mins, Total Time: 30 mins

Ingredients

- 2 (6 oz.) ((170g)) steaks, 3/4" thick rinsed and patted dry
- 1 teaspoon (5 ml) olive oil, to coat
- 1/2 teaspoon (0.5) garlic powder (optional)
- Salt, to taste
- Pepper, to taste
- Butter

Instructions

- Lightly coat steaks with olive oil. Season both sides of steaks with garlic powder (optional), salt, and pepper (we'll usually season liberally with salt & pepper).
- Preheat the Air Fryer at 400°F for 4 minutes.
- Air Fry for 400°F for 10-18 minutes, flipping halfway through (cooking time depends on how thick and cold the steaks are plus how do you prefer your steaks).
- If you want steaks to be cooked more, add additional 3-6 minutes of cooking time.
- Add a pat of butter on top of the steak, cover with foil, and allow the steak to rest for 5 minutes.
- Season with additional salt and pepper, if needed. Serve immediately.

Nutrition Facts

- Calories: 373kcal | Protein: 34g | Fat: 26g | Saturated Fat: 10g | Cholesterol: 103mg | Sodium: 88mg | Potassium: 455mg | Vitamin A: 25IU | Calcium: 12mg | Iron: 2.9mg

90. AIR FRYER STEAK BITES & MUSHROOMS

Prep Time: 10 mins

Cook Time: 18 mins

Total Time: 28 mins

Ingredients

- 1 lb. (454 g) steaks, cut into 1/2" cubes (ribeye, sirloin, tri-tip, or what you prefer)
- 8 oz. (227 g) mushrooms (cleaned, washed, and halved)
- 2 tablespoons (30 ml) butter, melted (or olive oil)
- 1 teaspoon (5 ml) worcestershire sauce
- 1/2 teaspoon (2.5 ml) garlic powder, optional
- Flakey salt, to taste
- Fresh cracked black pepper, to taste
- Minced parsley, garnish
- Melted butter, for finishing - optional
- Chili flakes, for finishing - optional
- **Instructions**
- Rinse and thoroughly pat dry the steak cubes. Combine the steak cubes and mushrooms. Coat with the melted butter and then season with Worcestershire sauce, optional garlic powder,

and a generous seasoning of salt and pepper.
- Preheat the Air Fryer at 400°F for 4 minutes.
- Spread the steak and mushrooms in an even layer in the air fryer basket. Air fry at 400°F for 10-18 minutes, shaking and flipping and the steak and mushrooms 2 times through the cooking process (time depends on your preferred doneness, the thickness of the steak, size of air fryer).
- Check the steak to see how well done it is cooked. If you want the steak more done, add an extra 2-5 minutes of cooking time.
- Garnish with parsley and drizzle with optional melted butter and/or optional chili flakes. Season with additional salt & pepper if desired. Serve warm.

Nutrition Facts

Calories: 401kcal | Carbohydrates: 3g | Protein: 32g | Fat: 29g | Saturated Fat: 14g | Cholesterol: 112mg | Sodium: 168mg | Potassium: 661mg | Sugar: 1g | Vitamin A: 255IU | Vitamin C: 1.6mg | Calcium: 11mg | Iron: 3.1mg

Air Fryer Vegetables Recipes

91. AIR FRYER ROAST VEGETABLES

Prep Time: 5 Minutes

Cook Time: 10 Minutes

Total Time: 15 Minutes

Ingredients

- 1 large sweet potato
- 1 large potato
- 1 large carrot
- ¼ small pumpkin
- ½ tsp spice or herb mix, optional

Instructions

- Wash the vegetables or peel if preferred, and cut into chunks no thicker than 1 inch (they can be as long as you like). Pat vegetables dry.
- Place vegetable pieces in an air fryer basket and spray with olive oil. Add spice if desired. Shake and spray with oil again.
- Cook in the air fryer at 360°F (180°C) for 5 minutes. Remove the basket and shake.
- Return to the air fryer and cook for a further 5-10 minutes until golden brown.

Nutrition Information

- Calories: 156| Unsaturated Fat: 0g| Sodium: 69mg| Carbohydrates: 35g| Fiber: 5g| Sugar: 6g| Protein: 4g

92. AIR FRYER ROASTED BRUSSELS SPROUTS

Prep Time: 5 Minutes

Cook Time: 18 Minutes

Total Time: 23 Minutes

Ingredients

- 1 pound Brussels sprouts
- 1 ½ tablespoon olive oil
- ½ teaspoon salt
- ½ teaspoon black pepper

Instructions

- Preheat the air fryer to 390 degrees.
- Wash Brussels sprouts and pat dry.
- Remove any loose leaves.
- If the sprouts are larger cut them in half.
- Place Brussels sprouts into a bowl.
- Drizzle olive oil over the vegetables.
- Stir to make sure the Brussels sprouts are fully coated. Place the Brussels sprouts in the basket.
- Season with salt and pepper.
- Cook for 15 to 18 minutes or until the Brussels sprouts soften and begin to brown.
- Serve immediately.

Nutrition Information

- Calories: 172 Total Fat: 11g Saturated Fat: 2g Unsaturated Fat: 9g Sodium: 577mg Carbohydrates: 16g Fiber: 6g Sugar: 4g Protein: 6g

93. AIR FRYER ROASTED BROCCOLI (LOW CARB + KETO)

Yield: 4

Cook Time: 8 Minutes

Total Time: 8 Minutes

Ingredients

- 5 cups broccoli florets
- 2 tablespoons butter
- 2 teaspoons minced garlic
- 1/3 cup shredded parmesan cheese
- Salt and pepper to taste
- Lemon slices (optional)

Instructions

- Melt the butter and combine with the minced garlic, set aside for later.
- Preheat your air fryer according to the manufactures directions at a temperature of 350 degrees.
- Add the chopped broccoli florets to the basket of the air fryer and spray very lightly with cooking oil.
- Roast the broccoli for 8 minutes total. I remove the basket after 4 minutes and shake or toss with tongs to make sure everything is cooking evenly, then cook for 4 more minutes.
- At this point, the broccoli should be fork tender at the thickest part of the stem and slightly crispy on the outside.
- Remove the broccoli from the basket and toss with the garlic butter, parmesan and add salt and pepper to taste.

Nutrition Information:

- Calories: 106| Total Fat: 7.9g| carbohydrates: 5.2g| fiber: 2.1g| protein: 5.3g

94. AIR-FRYER ROASTED VEGGIES

Prep Time: 20 mins

Cook Time: 10 mins

Total Time: 30 mins

Servings: 4

Ingredient

- ½ cup diced zucchini
- ½ cup diced summer squash
- ½ cup diced mushrooms
- ½ cup diced cauliflower
- ½ cup diced asparagus
- ½ cup diced sweet red pepper
- 2 teaspoons vegetable oil
- ¼ teaspoon salt
- ¼ teaspoon ground black pepper
- 1/4 teaspoon seasoning, or more to taste

Instructions

- Preheat the air fryer to 360 degrees F (180 degrees C).
- Add vegetables, oil, salt, pepper, and desired seasoning to a bowl. Toss to coat; arrange in the fryer basket.
- Cook vegetables for 10 minutes, stirring after 5

minutes.

Nutrition Facts

- Calories: 37| Protein: 1.4g| Carbohydrates: 3.4g| Fat: 2.4g| Sodium: 152.2mg

95. BUTTERY GARLIC GREEN BEANS

Prep Time: 10 mins

Cook Time: 10 mins

Total Time: 20 mins

Servings: 4

Ingredient

- 1 pound fresh green beans, trimmed and snapped in half
- 3 tablespoons butter
- 3 cloves garlic, minced
- 2 pinches lemon pepper
- Salt to taste

Instructions

- Place green beans into a large skillet and cover with water; bring to a boil. Reduce heat to medium-low and simmer until beans start to soften about 5 minutes. Drain water. Add butter to green beans; cook and stir until butter is melted 2 to 3 minutes.
- Cook and stir garlic with green beans until garlic is tender and fragrant for 3 to 4 minutes. Season with lemon pepper and salt.

Nutrition Facts

- Calories: 116; Protein: 2.3g; Carbohydrates: 8.9g; Fat: 8.8g; Cholesterol: 22.9mg; Sodium: 222.5mg

96. SUPERB SAUTEED MUSHROOMS

Prep Time: 10 mins

Cook Time: 15 mins

Total Time: 25 mins

Servings: 4

Ingredient

- 3 tablespoons olive oil
- 3 tablespoons butter
- 1 pound button mushrooms, sliced
- 1 clove garlic, thinly sliced
- 1 tablespoon red cooking wine
- 1 tablespoon teriyaki sauce, or more to taste
- ¼ teaspoon garlic salt, or to taste
- Freshly ground black pepper to taste

Instructions

- Heat olive oil and butter in a large saucepan over medium heat. Cook and stir mushrooms, garlic, cooking wine, teriyaki sauce, garlic salt, and black pepper in the hot oil and butter until mushrooms are lightly browned, about 5 minutes. Reduce heat to low and simmer until mushrooms are tender, 5 to 8 more minutes.

Nutrition Facts

- Calories: 199; Protein: 3.9g; Carbohydrates: 5.3g; Fat: 19.2g; Cholesterol: 22.9mg; Sodium:

97. PAN-FRIED ASPARAGUS

Prep Time: 5 mins

Cook Time: 15 mins

Additional Time: 5 mins

Total Time: 25 mins

Servings: 4

Ingredient

- ¼ cup butter
- 2 tablespoons olive oil
- 1 teaspoon coarse salt
- ¼ teaspoon ground black pepper
- 3 cloves garlic, minced
- 1 pound fresh asparagus spears, trimmed

Instructions

- Melt butter in a skillet over medium-high heat. Stir in the olive oil, salt, and pepper. Cook garlic in butter for a minute, but do not brown. Add asparagus, and cook for 10 minutes, turning asparagus to ensure even cooking.

Nutrition Facts

- Calories: 188; Protein 2.8g; Carbohydrates 5.2g; Fat

98. EASY ROASTED BROCCOLI

Prep Time: 10 mins

Cook Time: 20 mins

Total Time: 30 mins

Servings: 4

Ingredient

- 14 ounces broccoli
- 1 tablespoon olive oil
- Salt and ground black pepper to taste

Instructions

- Preheat oven to 400 degrees F (200 degrees C).
- Cut broccoli florets from the stalk. Peel the stalk and slice into 1/4-inch slices. Mix florets and stem pieces with olive oil in a bowl and transfer to a baking sheet; season with salt and pepper.
- Roast in the preheated oven until broccoli is tender and lightly browned, about 18 minutes.

Nutrition Facts

- Calories: 63| Protein: 2.8g| Carbohydrates: 6.5g| Fat: 3.7g| Sodium: 71.2mg.

99. AIR FRYER VEGGIES

Prep Time: 5 mins

Cook Time: 20 mins

Total Time: 25 mins

Ingredients

- 3 cups mixed vegetables, cut into 1-inch pieces (cauliflower, broccoli, squash, carrots, beets, etc)
- 1 tablespoon olive oil
- 1/2 teaspoon kosher salt

Preparation

- Place the vegetables in a bowl and toss to coat with the oil and salt.
- Place the vegetables in the air fryer basket and cook at 375F degrees for 15-20 minutes or until golden and fork-tender.

Nutrition Information

- Calories: 172
- Total Fat: 11g
- Sodium: 234mg
- Carbohydrates: 16g
- Fiber: 6g
- Sugar: 4g
- Protein: 6g

100. AIR FRYER "ROASTED" ASPARAGUS

Prep Time: 3 mins

Cook Time: 7 mins

Total Time: 10 mins

Servings: 4 servings

Ingredients

- 1 pound fresh asparagus, ends trimmed
- Oil spray or olive oil
- Salt, to taste
- Black pepper, to taste

Instructions

- Coat the asparagus with oil spray or olive oil and season with salt and pepper. Lay the asparagus evenly in the air fryer basket. Make sure to coat the asparagus tips so they don't burn or dry out too fast. It is best to season before you put it in the air fryer basket. Too much excess salt in the air fryer baskets will often start to break down with coating.
- Air Fry at 380°F for 7-10 minutes, depending on thickness, shake, and turn asparagus halfway through cooking.
- Taste for seasoning & tenderness, then serve.

Nutritional Value

- Calories: 572kcal | Carbohydrates: 1g | Protein: 46g | Fat: 43g | Saturated Fat: 22g | Cholesterol: 168mg | Sodium: 219mg | Potassium: 606mg | Sugar: 1g | Calcium: 16mg | Iron: 4mg

101. AIR FRYER VEGETABLES

Prep Time: 10 minutes

Cook Time: 10 minutes

Servings: 6

Ingredients

- 2 zucchini cut into dials
- 2 yellow squash cut into dials
- 1 container mushrooms cut in half
- 1/2 c olive oil
- 1/2 onion sliced
- 3/4 tsp Italian seasoning
- 1/2 tsp garlic salt
- 1/4 tsp Lawry's seasoned salt

Instructions

- Slice zucchini and yellow squash into dials. The thinner they are the softer they will get. I would recommend 3/4" thick so they all are the same consistency when done.
- Slice mushrooms in half. Put all vegetables in a bowl and toss together gently. (if you want to add 1/2-1 full precooked sausage link diced into bite-size pcs., add that now too)
- Pour olive oil on top and toss gently, then sprinkle in all seasonings in a bowl and gently toss one more time.
- Add half of your vegetables into your air fryer, close, and set to 400 degrees for 10 minutes. I did not bother shaking or tossing halfway through and they came out amazing.
- Remove, enjoy, and add another half at 400 degrees for 10 minutes to finish the cooking batch.

Nutrition Facts

- Fat: 18g Saturated Fat: 3g1 Sodium: 201mg Potassium: 355mg Carbohydrates: 5g Fiber: 2g Sugar: 3g

102. AIR FRYER FROZEN BROCCOLI, CARROTS, AND CAULIFLOWER – (GLUTEN-FREE, VEGAN, KETO, AND PALEO)

Prep time: 5 min

Cook time: 10 min

Total time: 15 min

Serves: 3 people

Ingredients:

- 3 cups frozen mixed broccoli, carrots, and cauliflower
- 1 TBS extra virgin olive oil
- 1 tsp Italian seasoning blend (or basil, oregano, rosemary, and thyme)
- 1/2 tsp nutritional yeast (optional)
- 1/2 tsp sea salt
- 1/4 tsp freshly cracked pepper

Directions:

- Preheat the air fryer to 375°F for 5 minutes.
- Place the frozen vegetables in a large mixing bowl. Pour the olive oil over the vegetables and toss to coat. Sprinkle the herbs, salt, pepper, and nutritional yeast over the vegetables and toss again.
- Add the vegetables to the crisper plate or basket of the air fryer in an even layer. Cook for 5 minutes. Shake the bucket, or rotate the vegetables. Continue to cook for an additional 4 to 6 minutes until the vegetables are tender and cooked through to a warm temperature. Taste one to test for doneness.
- Place the cooked vegetables on a serving platter. You can top with more nutritional yeast before serving.

Nutritional Value

- Total fat: 3.7g Sodium: 1820.8mg Sugar: 11.3g Vitamin A: 169.2ug Carbohydrates: 33.6mg Protein:18g Vitamin C: 165.5mg

103. HEALTHY AIR FRYER CHICKEN AND VEGGIES

Prep Time: 5 minutes
Cook Time: 15 minutes
Total Time: 20 minutes
Servings: 4 servings

Ingredients

- 1 pound chicken breast, chopped into bite-size pieces (2-3 medium chicken breasts)
- 1 cup broccoli florets (fresh or frozen)
- 1 zucchini chopped
- 1 cup bell pepper chopped (any colors you like)
- 1/2 onion chopped
- 2 cloves garlic minced or crushed
- 2 tablespoons olive oil
- 1/2 teaspoon EACH garlic powder, chili powder, salt, pepper
- 1 tablespoon Italian seasoning (or spice blend of choice)

Instructions

- Preheat air fryer to 400F.
- Chop the veggies and chicken into small bite-size pieces and transfer to a large mixing bowl.
- Add the oil and seasoning to the bowl and toss to combine.
- Add the chicken and veggies to the preheated air fryer and cook for 10 minutes, shaking halfway, or until the chicken and veggies are charred and chicken is cooked through. If your air fryer is small, you may have to cook them in 2-3 batches.

Nutrition

- Calories: 230kcal | Carbohydrates: 8g | Protein: 26g | Fat: 10g | Saturated Fat: 2g | Cholesterol: 73mg |

Air Fryer Meatless Recipes

104. GARLIC AND HERB ARTISAN BREAD

Prep Time: 2 hrs

Cook Time: 20 mins

Ingredients

- 1 cup water about 95F (35C)
- 1/2 tablespoon instant dry yeast
- 1/2 tablespoon salt
- 2 1/4 cup all-purpose flour
- 2 teaspoon garlic powder or to taste
- 1/2 teaspoon onion powder
- 1 teaspoon thyme
- 1/2 teaspoon dried parsley

Instructions

- In a medium bowl, gently stir the water and yeast.
- In a large mixing bowl, combine all dry ingredients and mix well.
- Pour the yeast and water mixture into the mixing bowl containing the dry ingredients and mix well. Cover the mixing bowl with a damp towel and let rise for about 2 hours or until the dough rose and double in size.
- Line a 7-inch cake barrel with parchment paper. Sprinkle a little flour onto the parchment paper.
- Use a spatula to punch down the dough then transfer the dough to the cake barrel. Sprinkle some flour on top and let it rise for about 30 minutes.
- If the air fryer you use has a detachable basket, pour about 3 tablespoons of water into the bottom of the outer basket. Preheat the air fryer at 400F (200C) for about 4 minutes.
- Put the cake barrel inside the fryer basket and air fryer at 400F (200C) for about 10-12 minutes until the bread has a nice golden-brown crust.
- Turn the bread over and air fry again at 400F (200C) for another 4-6 minutes until the crust is golden brown. Try knocking on the bread, if it sounds hollow then it is cooked through on the inside.
- Let cool on a wired rack for about 10-15 minutes before slicing.

Nutrition

Calories: 176kcal | Carbohydrates: 37g | Protein: 5g | Fat: 1g | Saturated Fat: 1g | Sodium: 585mg | Potassium: 62mg | Fiber: 1g | Sugar: 1g | Vitamin C: 1mg | Calcium: 7mg | Iron: 2mg

105. SOY AND ONION SUGAR SNAP PEAS

Prep Time: 3 mins

Cook Time: 7 mins

Ingredients

- 1 tablespoon melted butter
- 2 tablespoon finely chopped onion
- 2 teaspoon minced garlic
- 1/2 tablespoon soy sauce
- 1/2 teaspoon onion powder
- 1/4 teaspoon black pepper or to taste
- 8 ounces sugar snap peas (about 250g)

Instructions

- Remove and discard the stem end and string from each pea pod.
- In a cake barrel, mix butter, onion, and garlic. Air fry at 380F (190C) for 2 minutes.
- Add in sugar snap peas and the rest of the ingredients. Stir to make sure the snap peas are coated with butter.
- Air fry at 360F (180C) for about 5-7 minutes, stirring once in the middle.

Nutrition

- Calories: 56kcal | Carbohydrates: 6g | Protein: 2g | Fat: 3g | Saturated Fat: 2g | Cholesterol: 8mg | Sodium: 154mg | Potassium: 113mg | Fiber: 2g | Sugar: 3g | Vitamin C: 35mg | Calcium: 27mg | Iron: 1mg

106. KOREAN BBQ CHICKPEAS

Prep Time: 5 mins

Cook Time: 25 mins

Ingredients

- 1 can of garbanzo (chickpeas) beans drained
- 2 tablespoon Korean BBQ sauce
- 1/2 teaspoon gochujang Korean hot pepper paste or to taste
- 1/2 teaspoon honey

Instructions

- Line the fryer basket with a sheet of lightly greased aluminum foil.
- In a medium-sized bowl, mix the Korean BBQ sauce, gochujang, and honey until homogenous.
- Add in the garbanzo beans. Gently mix everything until all the beans are coated with the sauce.
- Transfer all the garbanzo beans and the sauce in the bowl to the fryer basket. Spread the beans out so they are not stacked on top of each other.
- Air fry at 320F (160C) for 23-25 minutes, string a few times in the middle until the sauce on the bean's surface caramelized.
- Let cool for about 5 minutes before serving.

Nutrition

- Calories: 190kcal | Carbohydrates: 33g | Protein: 10g | Fat: 3g | Saturated Fat: 1g | Sodium: 147mg | Potassium: 309mg | Fiber: 8g | Sugar: 8g | Vitamin C: 1mg | Calcium: 52mg | Iron: 3mg

107. AIR FRYER ROASTED ASPARAGUS

Prep Time5 mins

Cook Time10 mins

Total Time15 mins

Ingredients

- 1 bunch fresh asparagus
- 1 tablespoon olive oil or olive oil cooking spray
- salt and pepper to taste

- 1 1/2 teaspoons Herbes de Provence seasoning optional
- fresh lemon wedge optional

Instructions

- Wash and trim hard ends off asparagus.
- Drizzle the asparagus with olive oil and the seasonings. You can also use cooking oil spray.
- Add the asparagus to the air fryer.
- Cook for 6-10 minutes on 360 degrees until crisp. Drizzle fresh squeezed lemon over the roasted asparagus.
- I don't recommend going over 10 minutes in the air fryer. Monitor the asparagus closely because every air fryer brand cooks differently. I like for my roasted asparagus to have a little bit of char, but I don't want it to be too slimy. If you roast it too long you will burn it and will become really soft to the touch.
- After the asparagus has cooked for 5 minutes, start to monitor it closely.

108. EASY AIR FRYER BREAKFAST SCRUMBLED EGGS

Prep Time: 5 min

Cook Time: 10 min

Total Time: 15 minutes

Yield: 4 servings

Ingredients

- 4 eggs
- ½ cup shredded sharp cheddar cheese
- ¼ cup fresh spinach, chopped
- 2 scallions, chopped
- 2 tablespoons half and half
- salt and pepper to taste

Instructions

- In a medium bowl, beat eggs with half and half.
- Stir in cheese, spinach, scallions, salt, and pepper.
- Spray a 6" cake pan with cooking spray (very important). Pour mixture into the pan.
- Air fry at 350 degrees (F) for 10-14 minutes. A toothpick inserted will come out clean when done.

Nutritional Value

- Calories:178Kcal|Totalfat:15g|Saturatedfat:8g| Transfat:12g|Cholesterol:194mg|Sodium: 193mg|Carbohydrates: 2g|Sugar: 1g|Protein: 5g| Iron: 0.8mg| Calcium: 25mg

109. EASY ROASTED ASPARAGUS

Prep Time: 5 mins

Cook Time: 8 mins

Ingredients

- 1 pound asparagus ends trimmed (about 500g)
- 1/4 tsp sea salt or to taste
- 1/8 teaspoon black pepper or to taste
- 1 tablespoon extra virgin olive oil

Instructions

- Rinse the asparagus and drain.
- Put the asparagus on a large plate and drizzle olive oil on it and season with salt, pepper. Mix gently.
- Line the fryer basket with a grill mat or a sheet of lightly greased aluminum foil.
- Put the asparagus in the fryer basket, without stacking if possible, and air fry at 360F (180C) for about 6-8 minutes until tender.

Nutrition
- Calories: 54kcal | Carbohydrates: 4g | Protein: 3g | Fat: 4g | Saturated Fat: 1g | Sodium: 148mg | Potassium: 229mg | Fiber: 2g | Sugar: 2g |Vitamin C: 6mg | Calcium: 27mg | Iron: 2mg

110. BLUEBERRY CREAM CHEESE CROISSANT BAKE

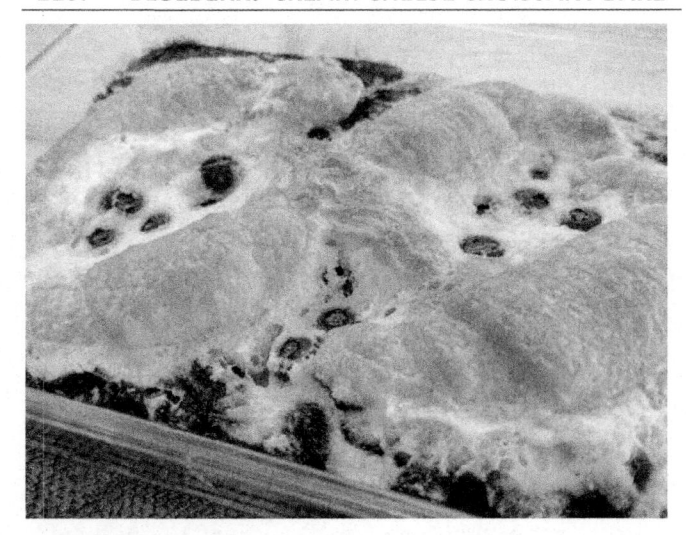

Prep Time: 10 mins

Cook Time: 20 mins

Ingredients
- 1/2 tube crescent dough (4 crescents) (or puff pastry sheets)
- 1/2 cup blueberry
- 4 oz cream cheese (約 113g)
- 1/3 cup sugar
- 1 egg
- 1/2 teaspoon vanilla
- 2 tablespoon milk

Instructions
- Roll the crescent dough into the shape of a crescent and set it aside.
- Lightly grease a shallow baking dish and set it aside.
- In an electric mixer, cream together cream cheese and sugar until fluffy.
- Add in milk, egg, and vanilla and mix until well combined and pour the mixture into the baking dish.
- Place the crescents on top and sprinkle the blueberries into the dish.
- Air fry at 280F (140C) for 18-20 minutes until the egg is set and the crescent rolls are golden brown.

Nutrition
- Calories: 206kcal | Carbohydrates: 22g | Protein: 4g | Fat: 12g | Saturated Fat: 6g | Cholesterol: 73mg | Sodium: 138mg | Potassium: 78mg | Fiber: 1g | Sugar: 20g | Vitamin C: 2mg | Calcium: 42mg | Iron: 1mg

Air Fryer Pork And Beef Recipes

111. MEATBALLS WITH GOCHUJANG MAYO

Prep Time: 15 mins

Cook Time: 10 mins

Ingredients

Ingredients For Meatballs:
- 1 pound ground pork (about 500g) or meat of your choice
- 1/4 cup onion finely chopped
- 2 Tablespoon soy sauce
- 2 teaspoon corn starch
- 1 teaspoon dried basil

- 1 teaspoon garlic powder
- 1 teaspoon onion powder
- 1/4 teaspoon white pepper powder

Ingredients For Sauce:

- 1 teaspoon Gochujang (Korean hot pepper paste)
- 2 Tablespoon Mayonnaise
- 2 Tablespoon mirin

Instructions

- Line the fryer basket with a grill mat or a sheet of lightly greased aluminum foil.
- Mix all the meatball ingredients then form them into about 1 inch balls. Put the meatballs in the fryer basket without stacking. Spray some oil onto the meatballs and air fry at 380F (190C) for 8-10 minutes until the meat is cooked through at its proper temperature.
- In the meantime, take a small bowl and mix all the sauce ingredients.
- Dip the meatballs in the Gochujang mayo to serve.

Nutrition

- Calories: 378kcal | Carbohydrates: 7g | Protein: 21g | Fat: 29g | Saturated Fat: 10g | Cholesterol: 85mg | Sodium: 677mg | Potassium: 368mg | Fiber: 1g | Sugar: 3g | Vitamin C: 2mg | Calcium: 21mg | Iron: 1mg

112. GENERAL TSO'S PORK

Prep Time: 15 mins
Cook Time: 20 mins

Ingredients For Pork:

- 1 pound pork shoulder cut into slices
- 1 egg beaten
- 2 Tablespoon soy sauce
- 1/4 teaspoon salt
- 1/4 teaspoon black pepper
- 1 teaspoon corn starch
- 1/4 cup tapioca starch
- Ingredients for sauce:
- 1 1/2 Tablespoon chili oil
- 2-3 Tablespoon minced garlic
- 1 Tablespoon grated ginger
- 2 Tablespoon soy sauce
- 2 Tablespoon vinegar
- 2 Tablespoon sugar
- 2 teaspoon corn starch mix with 4 teaspoon water

Instructions

- In a Ziploc bag, mix all the ingredients for the pork, except tapioca starch, and marinate in the refrigerator for at least one hour. Add the tapioca starch into the bag. Shake the bag or mix gently.
- Line the fryer basket with lightly greased aluminum foil. Put the pork slices in and spread them out as much as possible. Air fry at 400F (200C) for 15-17 minutes until the outside is crispy and the meat is cooked through, stir 2-3 times in between.
- In the meantime, use a saucepan to saute the garlic and ginger in chili oil for one minute. Add in the rest of the ingredients and bring them to a boil. Add in the corn starch and water mixture, stir until the sauce thickens.
- When the pork is done, toss in the sauce to coat. Sprinkle some chopped green onion to serve.

Nutrition

- Calories: 235kcal | Carbohydrates: 16g | Protein: 17g | Fat: 11g | Saturated Fat: 3g | Cholesterol: 87mg | Sodium: 1220mg | Potassium: 305mg | Fiber: 1g | Sugar: 6g | Vitamin A: 59IU | Vitamin C: 2mg | Calcium: 23mg | Iron: 2mg

113. KOREAN MARINATED PORK BELLY

Prep Time: 35 mins

Cook Time: 15 mins

Ingredients

- 1 pound pork belly with or without skin, (about 500g) cut into thin slices
- 2 Tablespoon minced garlic
- 2 Tablespoon minced ginger
- 1/2 tablespoon Korean hot pepper paste Gochujang, or to taste
- 3 tablespoon honey
- 3 tablespoon soy sauce
- 1 tablespoon sesame oil
- 1/2 tablespoon apple cider vinegar
- 3 tablespoon toasted white sesame seeds

Instructions

- Prepare the marinade by mixing all other ingredients. Use 3/4 of the marinade to marinate the pork belly for at least 30 minutes and save the rest for later use.
- On a lightly greased aluminum foil, air fry the pork belly slices at 380F (190C) for about 12 minutes, stir about 2 times in between, until the meat is cooked through.
- In the meantime, use a saucepan to heat the remaining marinade on the stovetop. Stir constantly until the sauce thickens. When the pork is done, toss with the sauce.
- To serve, sprinkle some sesame seeds and garnish with cilantro leaves or chopped green onion.

Nutrition

- Calories: 360kcal | Carbohydrates: 9g | Protein: 7g | Fat: 33g | Saturated Fat: 11g | Cholesterol: 41mg | Sodium: 397mg | Potassium: 149mg | Fiber: 1g | Sugar: 7g | Vitamin C: 1mg | Calcium: 37mg | Iron: 1mg

114. KOREAN STYLE PORK CHOPS

Prep Time: 3 hrs

Cook Time: 15 mins

Ingredients

- 1 pound pork chops (about 500g)
- 1/2 cup soy sauce
- 1/3 cup brown sugar
- 1/3 cup onion thinly sliced
- 2 Tablespoon grated ginger
- 2 Tablespoon minced garlic
- 2 teaspoon sesame oil
- 1 teaspoon black pepper
- 1-2 teaspoon Sriracha hot sauce optional
- 3 Tablespoon sliced green onions
- 1 Tablespoon toasted sesame seeds

Instructions

- Marinate the pork chops in all the ingredients (except sesame seeds and green onion) in the refrigerator for at least 3 hours. Take the pork chops out of the refrigerator about 30 minutes before air frying.
- Put the pork chops in the parchment paper-lined fryer basket without stacking. Air fry at 380F (190C) for about 15 minutes until the meat temperature is at least 165F (64C).
- Sprinkle some green onion and sesame seeds to serve.

Nutrition

- Calories: 309kcal | Carbohydrates: 24g | Protein: 28g | Fat: 11g | Saturated Fat: 3g | Cholesterol: 76mg | Sodium: 1709mg | Potassium: 581mg | Fiber: 1g | Sugar: 19g | Vitamin C: 4mg | Calcium: 62mg | Iron: 2mg

115. CHAR SIU PORK CHOPS

Prep Time: 3 hrs

Cook Time: 15 mins

Ingredients

- 1 pound pork chop about 500g
- 1/3 cup of store-bought char siu sauce see notes for substitution
- 2 Tablespoon soy sauce

Instructions

- Marinate the pork chops in all the ingredients. Refrigerate for at least 3 hours. Take the pork chops out of the refrigerator 30 minutes before air frying.
- Place the pork chops in the parchment paper-lined fryer basket and air fry at 380F (190C) for about 15 minutes until the meat temperature is at least 165F (64C).

Nutrition

- Calories: 206kcal | Carbohydrates: 7g | Protein: 25g | Fat: 8g | Saturated Fat: 3g | Polyunsaturated Fat: 1g | Monounsaturated Fat: 1g | Trans Fat: 1g | Cholesterol: 76mg | Sodium: 1032mg | Potassium: 442mg | Fiber: 1g | Sugar: 1g | Calcium: 8mg | Iron: 1mg

116. WASABI LIME STEAK

Prep Time: 1 hr 15 mins

Cook Time: 15 mins

Ingredients for the steak:

- 1 pound flank steak (about 500g) thinly sliced
- 1 tablespoon wasabi paste
- 2 Tablespoon soy sauce
- 2 Tablespoon lime juice
- 1/2 Tablespoon Sesame oil
- 1 Tablespoon grated ginger

Wasabi Mayonnaise:

- 1/4 cup mayonnaise
- 1 Tablespoon water
- 1 Tablespoon mirin non-alcohol
- 1 Tablespoon lime juice
- 1 teaspoon wasabi paste
- Other ingredients:
- 1/3 cup cilantro chopped

Instructions

- Combine all the ingredients for the steak and mix well. Marinate for at least one hour or overnight in the refrigerator.
- Line the fryer basket with a sheet of lightly greased aluminum foil. Spread the beef slices out as much as possible and air fry at 380F (190C) for about 8-10 minutes, stir 1-2 times in between.
- In the meantime, mix the mayonnaise, water, mirin, lime juice, and wasabi paste in a medium bowl.
- Drizzle the wasabi mayo over the steak and garnish with some cilantro to serve.

Nutrition

- Calories: 288kcal | Carbohydrates: 5g | Protein: 26g | Fat: 18g | Saturated Fat: 4g | Cholesterol: 74mg | Sodium: 686mg | Potassium: 427mg | Fiber: 1g | Sugar: 2g | Vitamin C: 6mg | Calcium: 29mg |

117. KOREAN BEEF WITH VEGGIE

Prep Time: 40 mins

Cook Time:15 mins

Ingredients For Beef:

12 ounces flank steak cut into thin slices

1 teaspoon corn starch

1/4 cup Korean BBQ sauce

Other Ingredients:

- 2 cups mung bean sprouts
- 3 cups baby spinach or spinach cut into 2-inch

length
- 1 Tablespoon sesame oil
- 1 Tablespoon minced garlic
- 1 Tablespoon freshly grated ginger
- 1 Tablespoon rice wine
- 2-3 Tablespoon Korean BBQ sauce
- 1 teaspoon jalapeno pepper sliced (optional)
- 1 teaspoon toasted sesame seeds

Instructions

- In a large bowl, marinate the beef with Korean BBQ sauce and corn starch for about 30 minutes.
- In a small pot, boil the mung bean sprouts until tender. Remove and set aside. Then, boil the spinach for about one minute and set aside.
- In a lightly greased cake pan, air fry the marinated beef at 380F (190C) for about 7-8 minutes, stir once in between.
- In the meantime, stir fry the garlic, grated ginger, and jalapeno pepper with sesame oil in a wok for about 1-2 minutes until fragrant. Add in the Korean BBQ sauce and rice wine and bring to a boil then turn the stove off.
- Toss the spinach, bean sprouts, and beef slices in the sauce. Sprinkle some sesame seeds over the dish to serve.

Nutrition

- Calories:220kcal | Carbohydrates: 13g | Protein: 22g | Fat: 8g | Saturated Fat: 2g | Cholesterol: 51mg | Sodium: 486mg | Potassium: 493mg | Fiber: 1g | Sugar: 9g | Vitamin C: 15mg | Calcium: 55mg | Iron: 2mg

118. MONGOLIAN BEEF

Prep Time: 15 mins

Cook Time: 10 mins

Ingredients For The Beef:

- 1 pound flank steak cut into 1/4 inch thick pieces (about 500g)
- 2 teaspoon soy sauce
- 1 teaspoon sesame oil
- 2 teaspoon cornstarch
- 1/4 cup tapioca starch

Ingredients For The Sauce:

- 2 Tablespoon olive oil
- 1 Tablespoon grated ginger
- 1 Tablespoon minced garlic
- 2 Tablespoon soy sauce
- 3 Tablespoon brown sugar
- 3-4 green onion green parts only, cut into 1-2 inch pieces
- 1-2 teaspoon sesame seeds optional

Instructions

- In a Ziploc back, marinate the steak pieces with soy sauce, sesame oil, and corn starch for at least 15 minutes. Add in the tapioca starch and shake, making sure all the pieces are coated.
- Line the fryer basket with a sheet of lightly greased aluminum foil. Put the steak pieces in, preferably without stacking, and air fry at 400F (200C) for about 8 minutes, flip once until the edges look slightly crispy.
- In the meantime, in a frying pan or a wok, saute the garlic and grated ginger in olive oil for about 1-2 minutes until fragrant. Add in the soy sauce and brown sugar and stir constantly until the sauce thickens.
- When the beef is done, toss the beef in the sauce, followed by the green onion. To serve, sprinkle the dish with sesame seeds if desired.

Nutrition

Calories: 306kcal | Carbohydrates: 19g | Protein: 26g | Fat: 14g | Saturated Fat: 4g | Cholesterol: 68mg | Sodium: 735mg | Potassium: 443mg | Fiber: 1g | Sugar: 9g | Vitamin A: 90IU | Vitamin C: 2mg | Calcium: 46mg | Iron: 2mg

119. FIVE SPICES SALT AND PEPPER PORK

Prep Time: 1 hr 15 mins

Cook Time: 15 mins

Ingredients

Ingredients For Pork:

- 1/2 pound pork shoulder cut into thick slices (about 250g)
- 2 Tablespoon soy sauce
- 1/2 Tablespoon rice wine
- 1 teaspoon corn starch
- 1 Tablespoon minced garlic
- 1 teaspoon sesame oil
- 1/2 teaspoon sugar
- 1/2 teaspoon Chinese five spices powder
- 1/4 cup tapioca starch

Instructions

- Marinate the meat with all the pork ingredients, except tapioca flour, for at least 1 hour.
- Dredge the pork slices in tapioca flour, shake off excess, and let sit for about 5-10 minutes until you don't see dry flour.
- Place the meat in the fryer basket and spray some oil. Air Fry at 380F for 12-14 minutes, flip once in the middle until the surface appears to be nice and crisp.
- Toss in the pork slices with chili pepper and chopped cilantro. Then, sprinkle some salt and pepper to serve.

Nutrition

- Calories: 100kcal | Carbohydrates: 9g | Protein: 8g | Fat: 3g | Saturated Fat: 1g | Cholesterol: 23mg | Sodium: 529mg | Potassium: 137mg | Fiber: 1g | Sugar: 1g | Vitamin C: 1mg | Calcium: 8mg | Iron: 1mg

120. SEASONED PORK CHOPS WITH AVOCADO SALSA

Prep Time: 5 mins

Cook Time: 15 mins

Ingredients

- 2 pork chops or pork shoulder blade steaks
- 2 Tablespoon olive oil
- 1 teaspoon sea salt
- 1 teaspoon black pepper
- 1/2 teaspoon paprika
- 1/2 teaspoon garlic powder
- 1/2 teaspoon cumin

Ingredients For Salsa:

- 1 avocado pitted and diced
- 1 large tomato seeded and diced
- 1/3 cup cilantro chopped
- 1 lime juiced
- 1/4 yellow onion finely chopped
- Pickled or fresh jalapeno to taste chopped (optional)
- Salt to taste

Instructions

- In a small bowl, mix all the dry seasonings in the pork ingredients and set them aside.
- Use a paper towel to pat dry the pork chop then rub both sides with olive oil. Generously season both sides of the meat and air fry at 380F (190C) for 10-12 minutes, flip once in the middle until the internal temperature exceeds 145F (63C).
- In the meantime, combine all the ingredients for the salsa in a large bowl.
- When the pork chops are done, let them rest for a few minutes. Scoop some salsa over the pork chops to serve.

Nutrition

- Calories: 528kcal | Carbohydrates: 18g | Protein: 32g | Fat: 38g | Saturated Fat: 7g |

Cholesterol: 90mg | Sodium: 1242mg | Potassium: 1187mg | Fiber: 9g | Sugar: 4g | Vitamin C: 30mg | Calcium: 39mg | Iron: 2mg

121. CHINESE STYLE GROUND MEAT PATTIES

Prep Time: 5 mins

Cook Time: 10 mins

Ingredients

- 1 pound ground pork about 500g
- 1 egg
- 1 teaspoon corn starch
- 1/3 cup green onion chopped
- 1/4 cup cilantro stems chopped
- 1/4 cup yellow onion finely diced
- 2 1/2 Tablespoon oyster sauce
- 2 Tablespoon minced garlic
- 1/4 teaspoon black pepper

Instructions

- Mix all the ingredients and making sure everything is well combined.
- Line the fryer basket with lightly greased aluminum foil. Form patties of equal size and place them into the fryer basket. Air fry at 380F (190C) for 8-10 minutes until fully cooked when the internal temperature exceeds 160F (72C).

Nutrition

- Calories: 335kcal | Carbohydrates: 5g | Protein: 21g | Fat: 25g | Saturated Fat: 9g | Cholesterol: 123mg | Sodium: 390mg | Potassium: 394mg | Fiber: 1g | Sugar: 1g | Vitamin C: 5mg |

122. PORK SATAY SKEWERS

Prep Time: 1 hr

Cook Time: 15 mins

Ingredients

Ingredients For Pork:

- 1 pound pork shoulder (about 500g) cut into 1/2 inch cubes
- 1/4 cup soy sauce
- 2 Tablespoons brown sugar
- 2 tablespoons Thai sweet chili sauce
- 1 Tablespoon sesame oil
- 1 Tablespoon minced garlic
- 1 Tablespoon fish sauce

Ingredients For The Sauce:

- 1/3 cup peanut butter
- 3 Tablespoon coconut milk or milk or water
- 2 Tablespoon Thai Sweet Chili Sauce
- 2 teaspoon minced garlic
- 2 teaspoon brown sugar
- 1 teaspoon fish sauce

Instructions

- Combine all the ingredients for the pork and marinate for at least 1 hour or overnight.
- In the meantime, soak the wooden skewers in water for at least 15 minutes. Also, combine all the ingredients for the dipping sauce and set aside.
- Thread the pork cubes onto skewers and place them in the fryer basket. Air fry at 380F (190C) for about 8-10 minutes, flip once in between until the meat is cooked through.

Nutrition

- Calories: 363kcal | Carbohydrates: 23g | Protein: 21g | Fat: 22g | Saturated Fat: 7g | Cholesterol: 46mg | Sodium: 1607mg | Potassium: 444mg | Fiber: 1g | Sugar: 18g | Vitamin C: 2mg | Calcium: 33mg | Iron: 2mg

Salad

123. AIR FRYER BUFFALO SALMON SALAD

Total Time: 30 mins

Ingredients

- 4 Tbsp. unsalted butter
- ¼ cup hot sauce
- 4 Verlasso salmon fillets (about 1 lb.)
- Cooking spray
- 1 large head romaine lettuce, chopped (about 8 cups)
- 1 ear of corn, kernels removed (or ½ cup frozen corn, thawed)
- ½ cup matchstick carrots
- 1 small red onion, thinly sliced
- 1 bell pepper, thinly sliced
- 3 stalks celery, chopped
- ¼ cup blue cheese crumbles
- Ranch or blue cheese dressing for serving, optional
- Additional hot sauce for serving, optional

Directions

- Melt butter in a small saucepan over medium heat. Remove pan from heat and stir in hot sauce.
- Place salmon in a baking pan and pour the sauce over salmon. Let marinate for 20-30 minutes, turning once halfway through.
- Preheat air fryer to 400°F. Lightly spray the fryer basket with cooking spray. Remove salmon from marinade and pat bottom (skin) dry. Place salmon in basket, skin side down, and cook for 7-10 minutes, or until salmon is cooked to desired doneness.
- While salmon is cooking, assemble the salad. Divide the lettuce among four bowls. Top each bowl with corn, carrots, onion, bell pepper, celery, and blue cheese. Place a salmon fillet on top of each salad.
- Drizzle with dressing and additional hot sauce if desired. Enjoy!

Nutrition

- Calories 360| Total Fat 22g|Cholesterol: 100mg| Sodium: 570mg|

124. GRILLED ROMAINE SALAD

Prep Time: 15 mins

Cook Time: 10 mins

Servings: 4 servings

Ingredients

- 2 medium heads of romaine lettuce, cut lengthwise into wedges
- Olive oil for brushing the romaine lettuce
- 1/2 cup crumbled or grated cheese (choose your favorite!)
- Lemon wedges for serving and squeezing over salad

For The Dressing

- 2 cloves garlic, crushed or fine mince
- 3 tablespoons olive oil for the dressing
- Zest of 1 fresh lemon
- 2 tablespoons fresh lemon juice
- 1 tablespoon balsamic vinegar
- 1/2 teaspoon dijon mustard
- 1 teaspoon soy sauce (use tamari for gluten free)
- 1 teaspoon brown sugar
- 1/2 teaspoon paprika
- 1/2 teaspoon kosher salt, or to taste
- Black pepper to taste

Instructions

Make The Dressing

- Whisk together the dressing ingredients (garlic, olive oil, lemon zest, lemon juice, balsamic, mustard, soy sauce, brown sugar, paprika, salt,

and black pepper). Set aside.
- Heat the grill to medium-high to high heat (depending on the grill's heat intensity). Make sure to scrape the grill grates so they are clean & food won't stick as easily.
- Lightly coat the romaine lettuce heads with oil. Grill the romaine until they're gently cooked and slightly charred.
- Allow grilled romaine to cool. Lay on a serving tray, drizzle dressing on top, and sprinkle with cheese. Serve with lemon wedges and enjoy!

Nutrition
- Calories: 165kcal | Carbohydrates: 4g | Protein: 4g | Fat: 15g | Saturated Fat: 4g | Cholesterol: 15mg | Sodium: 472mg | Potassium: 48mg | Fiber: 1g | Sugar: 2g | Vitamin C: 4mg | Calcium: 109mg | Iron: 0.3mg

125. SESAME GINGER SALMON WITH SPICY CUCUMBER SALAD

Prep time: 10mins

Cook time: 8mins

Ingredients
- 1/3 cup Annie's Organic Sesame Ginger Vinaigrette
- 1 pound salmon, cut into 4 portions
- 2 hothouse cucumbers, thinly sliced
- 1 jalapeño, thinly sliced
- A handful of fresh mint leaves, chopped
- 1/2 cup seasoned rice vinegar
- 1/2 teaspoon salt
- 1 teaspoon sugar

Method
- Pour ¼ cup Annie's Sesame Ginger Vinaigrette into the bottom of a medium bowl or baking dish
- Marinate salmon portions skin side facing up in dish for 5 minutes
- Mix cucumber slices, hot pepper, mint, vinegar, salt, + sugar in a large mason jar or medium bowl. Chill cucumber salad in the refrigerator, stirring every 5 minutes while salmon is cooking.
- After salmon has marinated for 5 minutes, place skin side down in air fryer
- Air Fry at 400°F for 8 minutes
- Drizzle salmon with remaining vinaigrette and air fry an additional 1-2 minutes until cooked through, browned, and crispy on the edges
- Using a slotted spoon to eliminate excess pickling juices, place ¼ cucumber salad topped with 1 salmon portion on each plate. Serve immediately!

Nutrient Value
- Calories: 122| Fat: 8g| Sat fat: 2g| Unsatfat: 5g| Protein: 10g| Carbohydrate| 0g Fiber 0g| Sugars 0g| Added sugars: 0g| Sodium:

126. AIR FRYER SqUASH WITH KALE SALAD

Prep Time: 5 minutes

Cook Time: 10 minutes

Total Time: 15 minutes

Ingredients
- Squash
- 1 medium delicata squash (see note 1)
- Salt and pepper to taste (or other spices)
- Salad
- 8 oz kale or other green, chopped
- 1 cup grape or cherry tomatoes, halved
- 2 cups cucumber, sliced
- 1/2 cup pomegranate seeds
- 1/4 cup squash seeds, roasted, optional
- 1/2 avocado, sliced, optional
- 1/2 cup vegan honey mustard dressing, or any dressing

Instructions

Cut The Squash: If using delicata, cut the top and

bottom off, then slice it lengthwise down the middle. Cut the delicata (or other squash) into half-inch thick pieces. You can leave delicate in a half-ring shape, or you can slice it into smaller pieces (especially if feeding littles) (bigger is fine, but will take longer to cook). If you find the squash hard to cut, try microwaving it for a minute or two first.

Save The Seeds: I highly recommend saving the seeds and roasting them! It's so easy, and worth it. I find it easiest to scoop out the seeds and membrane with a grapefruit spoon. Then fill a medium-sized bowl with water, so that the seeds mostly float to the top as I free them from the membrane.

Season: Lightly spray the squash with water, (or oil, if that's your thing) and season with salt, pepper, and whatever else you like (sometimes I use garlic, chili, etc.)

Air Fryer Method: Add to your air fryer. They will get crispier if they are in a single layer. Air fry at 375 degrees F (or 191 degrees C) for about 10 minutes, shaking halfway through. If you like it more browned, you can keep cooking for another 5 minutes or so.

Oven Method: Line a baking tray with a silicone baking mat or parchment paper. Lay the squash pieces out in a single layer with a little breathing room (about an inch) between each piece. Bake at 400 degrees Fahrenheit (or 205 degrees Celsius) for about 20-25 minutes, flipping the pieces halfway through.

Store: Refrigerate leftovers in an airtight container. The salad will keep for about 3 days (if dressed), the squash about 5 days (keep separate from the salad if possible). The seeds should keep on the counter in an airtight container for about 5 days.

Nutrients Value

- Calories: 213
- Total Fat: 5.2g
- Sodium: 419.8mg
- Sugar: 23.6g
- Carbohydrates: 37.1mg
- Protein: 7.1g
- Vitamin C: 165.5mg Citrus & Avocado Salad

Prep Time: 10 Mins

Total Time: 10 minutes

Ingredients

- 1/2 red grapefruit
- 1 blood orange
- 1 Navel orange
- 1/2 avocado
- 1/4 cup chopped roasted pistachios
- 2 Tbsp. chives
- 1 Tbsp. blood orange infused olive oil
- Sea salt & black pepper to taste!

Instructions

- Slice all citrus in whole circular thin slices.
- Arrange citrus on a large plate and top with avocado slices.
- Garnish with chopped chives, pistachios, blood orange olive oil, sea salt, and pepper.

Nutrient Value

- Total Fat: 22g| Saturated Fat: 10g| Trans Fat: 0g| Unsaturated Fat: 12g| Cholesterol: 88mg| Sodium: 789mg| Carbohydrates: 2g| Fiber: 1g| Sugar: 0g| Protein: 29g

127. RADICCHIO SALAD WITH CASHEW RICOTTA DRESSING

Prep Time: 10 Minutes

Cook Time: 20 Minutes

Total Time: 30 Minutes

Dressing

- 1/2 cup raw cashews, soaked in hot water for 10 minutes (or sub unroasted macadamia nuts)
- 2 cloves garlic
- 2 Tbsp lemon juice
- 1 ½ Tbsp nutritional yeast
- 1/3 tsp sea salt, plus more to taste
- 1 dash onion powder (optional)
- Water to thin

Beets

- 1 medium beet, thinly sliced into rounds
- 7 cloves garlic, peeled + roughly chopped
- 1 tsp avocado oil (if oil-free, sub maple syrup)
- 1 healthy pinch of each sea salt and black pepper

Candied Walnuts

- 2/3 cup raw walnuts
- 2 tsp maple syrup
- 1 ½ tsp coconut sugar
- 1 pinch sea salt
- 1 dash ground cinnamon

Salad

- 1 head radicchio, rinsed, dried, bottom trimmed, unpeeled, and roughly chopped (~6 cups as the recipe is written)
- 1/2 medium lemon, juiced
- 1 healthy pinch of each sea salt and black pepper
- 1/2 cup chopped fresh parsley

Instructions

- Heat oven to 425 degrees F (218 C) and line a baking sheet with parchment paper.
- Add cashews to a small bowl and cover with very hot water. Soak for 10 minutes.
- Add sliced beets and chopped garlic to the prepared baking pan and toss in a bit of oil and salt and pepper. Roast for 10-15 minutes, or until the beets are caramelized and the garlic is golden brown (being careful not to burn).
- In the meantime, add walnuts to a skillet (we prefer cast iron) and heat over medium heat to toast for 5 minutes, stirring frequently, being careful not to burn. Then add maple syrup, coconut sugar, salt, and cinnamon and toss to combine. Turn off heat and allow to cool in the pan.
- In the meantime, prepare the dressing. Drain cashews and add to a small blender (we use this small spice grinder that also has a cup for blending small-batch sauces) along with other dressing ingredients.
- Taste and adjust flavor as needed, adding more garlic for zing, lemon for acidity, salt to taste, or nutritional yeast for cheesiness. It should be zingy, salty, and lemony with a bit of cheesiness. It needs to be quite flavorful, so don't be shy!
- Add radicchio to a serving bowl or platter and toss with lemon juice, salt, and pepper. Then add cashew dressing and toss to coat.
- Top with roasted beets, garlic, and candied walnuts. Garnish with fresh parsley. Serve.

Nutrition Value

- Calories: 274 Carbohydrates: 20.4 g Protein: 9 g Fat: 19.6 g Saturated Fat: 2.5 g Polyunsaturated Fat: 9.44 g Monounsaturated Fat: 6.2 g Trans Fat: 0 g Cholesterol: 0 mg Sodium: 286 mg Potassium: 579 mg Fiber: 4 g Sugar: 7.1 g Vitamin A: 660 IU Vitamin C: 23.46 mg Calcium: 67.4 mg Iron: 2.82 mg

128. AIR FRYER CROUTONS

Total Time: 30 mins

Ingredients

- 4 slices bread
- 2 tablespoons melted butter
- 1 teaspoon parsley
- 1/2 teaspoon onion powder
- 1/2 teaspoon seasoned salt
- 1/2 teaspoon garlic salt

Instructions

- Preheat the air fryer to 390 degrees.
- Cut 4 slices of bread into bite-sized pieces.
- Melt butter, and place butter into a medium-sized bowl.
- Add 1 teaspoon parsley, 1/2 teaspoon seasoned salt, 1/2 teaspoon garlic salt, 1/2 teaspoon of onion powder to the melted butter. Stir well.
- Add bread to the bowl and carefully stir to coat the bread so that it is coated by the seasoned butter.
- Place buttered bread into the air fryer basket.
- Cook for 5 to 7 minutes or until the bread is toasted.
- Serve immediately.

Nutrition Value

- Calories: 127kcal | Carbohydrates: 14g | Protein: 3g | Fat: 7g | Saturated Fat: 4g | Cholesterol: 15mg | Sodium: 777mg | Potassium: 51mg | Fiber: 1g | Sugar: 2g | Vitamin A: 175IU | Calcium: 39mg | Iron: 1mg

129. GRILLED ROMAINE SALAD

Prep Time: 10 Minutes

Cook Time: 2 Minutes

Total Time: 12 Minutes

Ingredients

- 2 heads of romaine lettuce
- 6 slices of bacon
- 6 oz. pomegranate seeds
- 6 oz. of blue cheese crumbles
- 12 oz. of blue cheese dressing (see recipe card below)
- 4 tbsp of olive oil
- 1 tbsp balsamic glaze

Instructions

- Cook the bacon in an air fryer at 370°F for 8-12 minutes until crispy and slice into crumbles. Check out the recipe for the best air fryer bacon.
- Slice the heads of romaine in half, lengthwise.
- Brush the romaine lettuce with olive oil.
- Place the romaine cut side down on the medium-hot grill.
- Flip the heads of romaine after 1-2 minutes and cook on for equal time on the other side.
- Transfer the romaine cut side up to a serving platter and pile on the bacon, pomegranate seeds, and blue cheese crumbles.
- Finish by drizzling the amazing blue cheese salad dressing over the grilled romaine (see recipe below)
- Drizzle with a sweet balsamic glaze, and serve.

Nutrition Information

- Total Fat: 51g Saturated Fat: 13g Trans Fat: 1g Unsaturated Fat: 36g Cholesterol: 50mg Sodium: 901mg
- Carbohydrates: 17g Fiber: 6g Sugar: 10g Protein: 14g

130. FRIED CHICKPEAS IN THE AIR FRYER

Prep Time: 2 minutes

Cook Time: 12 minutes

Total Time: 14 minutes

Ingredients

- 1 1/2 cups chickpeas 1 15 ounces can drain & rinse
- Spritz cooking spray
- 2 teaspoons nutritional yeast flakes
- 1/2 teaspoon granulated onion
- Pinch salt

Instructions

- Put the drained chickpeas into the air fryer basket. Set the air fryer for 400 degrees and 12 minutes.
- Cook the plain chickpeas for the first 5 minutes. This will dry them out.
- Then open the basket, spritz the chickpeas with oil, give a shake, and spritz them again. Sprinkle on nutritional yeast flakes, granulated onion, and a pinch of salt.
- Return the basket to the air fryer and cook for the remaining 7 minutes.
- Test a chickpea to see if it's done enough for you. Depending on your air fryer, the softness of your chickpeas, and your personal preferences, you may want to cook them for an additional 3 to 5 minutes. If desired, add another pinch of salt before serving.

Nutrition

- Calories: 105kcal | Carbohydrates: 17g | Protein: 5g | Fat: 1g | Sodium: 4mg | Potassium: 198mg | Fiber: 4g | Sugar: 2g | Vitamin A: 15IU | Vitamin C: 0.8mg | Calcium: 30mg | Iron: 1.8mg

131. AIR FRYER BUFFALO CHICKEN TENDERS SALAD

Prep Time: 15 minutes

Cook Time: 25 minutes

Total Time: 40 minutes

Ingredients

Chicken Tenders:

- ½ cup blanched almond flour
- 1 tsp sea salt
- 1 tsp paprika
- ¼ tsp ground black pepper
- 2 large chicken breasts, sliced lengthwise into ½" strips
- ¼ cup tapioca flour
- 2 tbsp garlic-infused olive oil
- Avocado oil cooking spray

Salad:

- 2 hearts of romaine, chopped
- 1 cup carrots, coarsely-shredded
- 1 cup grape tomatoes, halved
- 1 bunch scallions, green tops only, chopped
- 1 red pepper, diced
- Your other favorite salad ingredients

Ranch Dressing:

- ½ Batch of my dairy-free homemade ranch dressing recipe (paleo, whole30, low fodmap)

Buffalo Sauce:

- ⅓ cup Paleo Low-FODMAP hot sauce
- 3 tbsp ghee, melted
- 1 tbsp garlic-infused olive oil
- ½ tbsp coconut aminos

Instructions

- Preheat the air fryer to 370° F for 10 minutes. While your air fryer preheats, combine almond flour, sea salt, paprika, and pepper in a large bowl, whisk to combine, and set aside. Place chicken strips in another large bowl. Add tapioca flour to the bowl and toss with your hands to coat the strips evenly. Add the garlic-infused oil and toss again to coat. Dredge each strip in the almond flour mixture, shaking off the excess, and set on a plate.
- Once your air fryer has preheated, spray the pan with cooking spray. Using tongs, place half of the breaded chicken strips in the pan in one layer, ideally not touching one another. Spray the strips lightly with cooking spray. Air fry for 12 minutes, flipping halfway through. Once the first batch has cooked, place it on a clean plate using a clean set of tongs and set aside. Using tongs, take one of the thickest strips out of the air fryer and check its temperature using an instant-read thermometer. The temperature of cooked chicken should be at least 165° F (75° C) to be safely consumed. Once the first batch is at the proper temperature, repeat these steps for the second half of the strips.
- While the chicken strips are frying, prepare a half-batch of my dairy-free homemade ranch dressing recipe, cover, and refrigerate until ready to serve. Chop the ingredients under "salad," place in a large serving bowl, and refrigerate.
- A minute or two before the chicken strips are done, in a large bowl, add the ingredients under "buffalo sauce," whisk to combine, and set aside until all the chicken strips are cooked. If the sauce solidifies, microwave it (covered) for about 20 seconds and whisk again.
- Once the second batch of strips has finished cooking, if desired, place the first batch back in the air fryer on top of the second batch and air fry at 370° F for a minute or so until heated (I typically skip this step as they're going on a cold salad anyway). Using tongs, take each strip out of the air fryer, dip in the buffalo sauce until fully-coated, and place it on a plate. Chop strips horizontally into small pieces if desired and serve on top of the salad with the ranch dressing.

Nutrient Value

Total Fat: 30.8gg Sodium: 1321.9mg Sugar: 6.7g Vitamin A: 567.5ug Carbohydrates: 21.4g Protein:29.8g Vitamin C: 56.8mg

Seafood

132. SEARED SCALLOPS WITH JALAPENO VINAIGRETTE

Prep Time: 5 mins Cook Time: 10 mins Total Time: 15 mins

Servings: 4

Ingredient

- 1 large jalapeno pepper, seeded and membranes removed
- ¼ cup rice vinegar
- ¼ cup olive oil
- ¼ teaspoon dijon mustard
- Salt and freshly ground black pepper to taste
- 1 tablespoon vegetable oil
- 12 large fresh sea scallops
- 1 pinch sea salt
- 1 pinch cayenne pepper
- 2 oranges, peeled and cut in between sections as segments

Instructions

- Place jalapeno, rice vinegar, olive oil, and Dijon mustard in a blender. Puree on high until mixture is completely liquefied, 1 to 2 minutes. Season with salt and black pepper to taste.
- Season scallops with sea salt and cayenne pepper. Heat vegetable oil in a skillet over high heat. Place scallops in skillet and cook until browned, 2 to 3 minutes per side. Transfer to a plate. Garnish scallops with orange segments and drizzle jalapeno vinaigrette over the top.

Nutrition Facts

- Calories: 307; Protein 30.1g; Carbohydrates

5.9g; Fat 18g; Cholesterol 72.4mg; Sodium 472mg.

133. BAKED TILAPIA WITH DILL SAUCE

Prep Time: 10 mins Cook Time: 20 mins Total Time: 30 mins

Servings: 4

Ingredient

- 4 (4 ounce) fillets tilapia
- Salt and pepper to taste
- 1 tablespoon cajun seasoning, or to taste
- 1 lemon, thinly sliced
- ¼ cup mayonnaise
- ½ cup sour cream
- ⅛ teaspoon garlic powder
- 1 teaspoon fresh lemon juice
- 2 tablespoons chopped fresh dill

Instructions

- Preheat the oven to 350 degrees F (175 degrees C). Lightly grease a 9x13 inch baking dish.
- Season the tilapia fillets with salt, pepper, and Cajun seasoning on both sides. Arrange the seasoned fillets in a single layer in the baking dish. Place a layer of lemon slices over the fish fillets. I usually use about 2 slices on each piece so that it covers most of the surface of the fish.
- Bake uncovered for 15 to 20 minutes in the preheated oven, or until fish flakes easily with a fork.
- While the fish is baking, mix the mayonnaise, sour cream, garlic powder, lemon juice, and dill in a small bowl. Serve with tilapia.

Nutrition Facts

- Calories: 284; Protein 24.5g; Carbohydrates 5.7g; Fat 18.6g; Cholesterol 58.9mg; Sodium 500.5mg.

134. ANGY LEMON-GARLIC SHRIMP

Prep Time: 10 mins

Cook Time: 10 mins

Total Time: 20 mins

Servings: 4

Ingredient

- 16 large shrimp - peeled, deveined, and tails on, or more to taste
- 3 large cloves garlic, smashed, or more to taste
- 1 teaspoon crushed red pepper, or to taste
- 2 teaspoons seafood seasoning (such as old bay®), or to taste
- Salt and ground black pepper to taste
- 2 tablespoons lemon juice
- 3 tablespoons chopped fresh parsley
- 3 teaspoons lemon zest

Instructions

- Heat a large skillet over medium-low heat until warm, about 3 minutes. Add shrimp, garlic, and crushed red pepper all at once and stir together. Add seafood seasoning, salt, and black pepper. Mix everything.
- Cook over medium heat until shrimp are fully cooked, 3 to 5 minutes. Pour lemon juice into skillet and stir again. Reduce heat to low; add parsley and lemon zest. Transfer only shrimp to a serving platter.

Nutrition Facts

- Calories: 76; Protein 14.2g; Carbohydrates 2.4g; Fat 0.9g; Cholesterol 127.7mg; Sodium 460.3mg.

135. PARMESAN-CRUSTED SHRIMP SCAMPI WITH PASTA

Prep Time: 25 mins

Cook Time: 20 mins

Total Time: 45 mins

Servings: 6

Ingredient

- 2 cups angel hair pasta
- ½ cup butter, divided
- 4 cloves garlic, minced
- 1 pound uncooked medium shrimp, peeled and deveined
- ½ cup white cooking wine
- 1 lemon, juiced
- 1 teaspoon red pepper flakes
- ¾ cup seasoned bread crumbs
- ¾ cup freshly grated Parmesan cheese, divided
- 2 tablespoons finely chopped fresh parsley

Instructions

- Bring a large pot of lightly salted water to a boil. Cook angel hair pasta in the boiling water, stirring occasionally, until tender yet firm to the bite, 4 to 5 minutes. Drain and set aside.
- Set an oven rack about 6 inches from the heat source and preheat the oven's broiler.
- Heat 1/4 cup butter over medium heat in a large, deep skillet. Add garlic; cook and stir until fragrant. Add shrimp, white wine, and lemon juice; continue to cook and stir until shrimp is bright pink on the outside and the meat is opaque about 5 minutes. Stir in red pepper flakes until well combined. Remove from heat and set aside.
- Place remaining 1/4 cup butter, bread crumbs, 1/2 the Parmesan cheese, and parsley in a bowl. Stir until well combined. Set aside.
- Place cooked pasta into shrimp scampi mixture; toss until fully coated in sauce. Add remaining Parmesan cheese and toss well. Top with bread crumb mixture.
- Broil in the preheated oven until golden brown, 3 to 4 minutes. Serve immediately.

Nutrition Facts

- Calories: 419; Protein 22.6g; Carbohydrates 33.4g; Fat 20.8g; Cholesterol 164.7mg; Sodium 731.6mg

136. BEST TUNA CASSEROLE

Prep Time: 15 mins

Cook Time: 20 mins

Total Time: 35 mins

Servings: 6

Ingredient

- 1 (12 ounces) package egg noodles
- ¼ cup chopped onion
- 2 cups shredded Cheddar cheese
- 1 cup frozen green peas
- 2 (5 ounce) cans tuna, drained
- 2 (10.75 ounces) cans condensed cream of mushroom soup
- ½ (4.5 ounces) can sliced mushrooms
- 1 cup crushed potato chips

Instructions

- Bring a large pot of lightly salted water to a boil. Cook pasta in boiling water for 8 to 10 minutes, or until al dente; drain.
- Preheat oven to 425 degrees F (220 degrees C).
- In a large bowl, thoroughly mix noodles, onion, 1 cup cheese, peas, tuna, soup, and mushrooms. Transfer to a 9x13 inch baking dish, and top with potato chip crumbs and remaining 1 cup cheese.
- Bake for 15 to 20 minutes in the preheated oven, or until cheese is bubbly.

Nutrition Facts

- Calories: 595; Protein 32.1g; Carbohydrates 58.1g; Fat 26.1g; Cholesterol 99.2mg; Sodium 1061.1mg

137. GOOD NEW ORLEANS CREOLE GUMBO

Prep Time: 1 hr

Cook Time: 2 hrs 40 mins

Total Time: 3 hrs 40 mins

Servings: 20

Ingredient

- 1 cup all-purpose flour
- ¾ cup bacon drippings
- 1 cup coarsely chopped celery
- 1 large onion, coarsely chopped
- 1 large green bell pepper, coarsely chopped
- 2 cloves garlic, minced
- 1 pound andouille sausage, sliced
- 3 quarts water
- 6 cubes beef bouillon
- 1 tablespoon white sugar
- Salt to taste
- 2 tablespoons hot pepper sauce (such as tabasco®), or to taste
- ½ teaspoon cajun seasoning blend (such as tony chachere's), or to taste
- 4 bay leaves
- ½ teaspoon dried thyme leaves
- 1 (14.5 ounces) can stewed tomatoes
- 1 (6 ounces) can tomato sauce
- 4 teaspoons file powder, divided
- 2 tablespoons bacon drippings
- 2 (10 ounces) packages frozen cut okra, thawed
- 2 tablespoons distilled white vinegar
- 1 pound lump crabmeat
- 3 pounds uncooked medium shrimp, peeled and deveined
- 2 tablespoons worcestershire sauce

Instructions

- Make a roux by whisking the flour and 3/4 cup bacon drippings together in a large, heavy saucepan over medium-low heat to form a smooth mixture. Cook the roux, whisking constantly until it turns a rich mahogany brown color. This can take 20 to 30 minutes; watch heat carefully and whisk constantly or roux will burn. Remove from heat; continue whisking until the mixture stops cooking.
- Place the celery, onion, green bell pepper, and garlic into the work bowl of a food processor, and pulse until the vegetables are very finely chopped. Stir the vegetables into the roux, and mix in the sausage. Bring the mixture to a simmer over medium-low heat, and cook until vegetables are tender, 10 to 15 minutes. Remove from heat, and set aside.
- Bring the water and beef bouillon cubes to a boil in a large Dutch oven or soup pot. Stir until the bouillon cubes dissolve, and whisk the roux mixture into the boiling water. Reduce heat to a simmer, and mix in the sugar, salt, hot pepper sauce, Cajun seasoning, bay leaves, thyme, stewed tomatoes, and tomato sauce. Simmer the soup over low heat for 1 hour; mix in 2 teaspoons of file gumbo powder at the 45-minute mark.
- Meanwhile, melt 2 tablespoons of bacon drippings in a skillet, and cook the okra with vinegar over medium heat for 15 minutes; remove okra with a slotted spoon, and stir into the simmering gumbo. Mix in crabmeat, shrimp, and Worcestershire sauce, and simmer until

flavors have blended, 45 more minutes. Just before serving, stir in 2 more teaspoons of file gumbo powder.

Nutrition Facts

- Calories: 283; Protein 20.9g; Carbohydrates 12.1g; Fat 16.6g; Cholesterol 142.6mg; Sodium 853.1mg.

138. SHRIMP SCAMPI WITH PASTA

Prep Time: 20 mins

Cook Time: 20 mins

Total Time: 40 mins

Servings: 6

Ingredient

- 1 (16 ounces) package linguine pasta
- 2 tablespoons butter
- 2 tablespoons extra-virgin olive oil
- 2 shallots, finely diced
- 2 cloves garlic, minced
- 1 pinch red pepper flakes (optional)
- 1 pound shrimp, peeled and deveined
- 1 pinch kosher salt and freshly ground pepper
- ½ cup dry white wine
- 1 lemon, juiced
- 2 tablespoons butter
- 2 tablespoons extra-virgin olive oil
- ¼ cup finely chopped fresh parsley leaves
- 1 teaspoon extra-virgin olive oil, or to taste

Instruction

- Bring a large pot of salted water to a boil; cook linguine in boiling water until nearly tender, 6 to 8 minutes. Drain.
- Melt 2 tablespoons butter with 2 tablespoons olive oil in a large skillet over medium heat. Cook and stir shallots, garlic, and red pepper flakes in the hot butter and oil until shallots are translucent, 3 to 4 minutes. Season shrimp with kosher salt and black pepper; add to the skillet and cook until pink, stirring occasionally, 2 to 3 minutes. Remove shrimp from skillet and keep warm.
- Pour white wine and lemon juice into skillet and bring to a boil while scraping the browned bits of food off of the bottom of the skillet with a wooden spoon. Melt 2 tablespoons butter in a skillet, stir 2 tablespoons olive oil into butter mixture, and bring to a simmer. Toss linguine, shrimp, and parsley in the butter mixture until coated; season with salt and black pepper. Drizzle with 1 teaspoon olive oil to serve.

Nutrition Facts

- Calories: 511; Protein 21.9g; Carbohydrates 57.5g; Fat 19.4g; Cholesterol 135.4mg; Sodium 260mg.

139. EASY GARLIC-LEMON SCALLOPS

Prep Time: 10 mins

Cook Time: 10 mins

Total Time: 20 mins

Servings: 6

Ingredient

- ¾ cup butter
- 3 tablespoons minced garlic
- 2 pounds large sea scallops
- 1 teaspoon salt
- ⅛ teaspoon pepper
- 2 tablespoons fresh lemon juice

Instructions

- Melt butter in a large skillet over medium-high heat. Stir in garlic, and cook for a few seconds until fragrant. Add scallops, and cook for several minutes on one side, then turn over, and continue cooking until firm and opaque.
- Remove scallops to a platter, then whisk salt, pepper, and lemon juice into butter. Pour sauce over scallops to serve.

Nutrition Facts

- Calories: 408; Protein 38.5g; Carbohydrates 8.9g; Fat 24.4g; Cholesterol 152.4mg; Sodium 987.9mg.

Air Fryer Dessert And Snacks Recipes

140. PEANUT BUTTER CUPCAKE SWIRL

Prep Time: 10 mins

Cook Time: 15 mins

Ingredients

- 1/4 cup butter softened
- 1/3 cup creamy peanut butter
- 2 tbsp sugar
- 1 egg
- 3/4 cup milk
- 1/2 tsp vanilla extract
- 3/4 cup cake flour
- 1 tsp baking soda
- 1/2 tsp baking powder
- 1/2 tsp salt
- 1/4 cup Nutella divided warmed

Instructions

- Line the muffin tins with cupcake liners and set them aside.
- Cream together the butter, sugar, and peanut butter using a whisk or an electric mixer. Then, add the egg, milk, and vanilla extract. Mix until homogenous. Finally, add the rest of the dry ingredients and mix until well combined.
- Scoop the batter into the liners about 2/3 full. Then, use a spoon to drop about 1/2 teaspoon of Nutella into the center of the cupcake. Insert a toothpick into the center of the Nutella and create a swirl by making circles in the batter.
- Air fry at 300F (150C) for about 12-14 minutes. Insert a toothpick to test. When the toothpick comes out clean, then the cupcake is cooked through.

Nutrition

- Calories: 215kcal | Carbohydrates: 18g | Protein: 5g | Fat: 14g | Saturated Fat: 7g | Cholesterol: 34mg | Sodium: 378mg | Potassium: 168mg | Fiber: 1g | Sugar: 9g | Calcium: 54mg | Iron: 1mg

141. GLUTEN-FREE FRESH CHERRY CRUMBLE

Prep Time: 15 mins

Cook Time: 25 mins

Additional Time: 30 mins

Total Time: 1 hr 10 mins

Ingredient

- ⅓ cup butter
- 3 cups pitted cherries
- 10 tablespoons white sugar, divided
- 2 teaspoons lemon juice
- 1 cup gluten-free all-purpose baking flour
- 1 teaspoon vanilla powder
- 1 teaspoon ground nutmeg
- 1 teaspoon ground cinnamon

Instructions

- Cube butter and place in freezer until firm, about 15 minutes.
- Preheat air fryer to 325 degrees F (165 degrees C).
- Combine pitted cherries, 2 tablespoons sugar, and lemon juice in a bowl; mix well. Pour cherry mixture into baking dish.
- Mix flour and 6 tablespoons of sugar in a bowl. Cut in butter using fingers until particles are pea-size. Distribute over cherries and press down lightly.
- Stir 2 tablespoons sugar, vanilla powder, nutmeg, and cinnamon together in a bowl. Dust sugar topping over the cherries and flour.
- Bake in the preheated air fryer. Check at 25 minutes; if not yet browned, continue cooking and checking at 5-minute intervals until slightly browned. Close drawer and turn off air fryer. Leave crumble inside for 10 minutes. Remove and allow to cool slightly, about 5 minutes.

Nutrition Facts

- Calories: 459| Protein: 4.9g| Carbohydrates: 76.4g| Fat: 17.8g| Cholesterol: 40.7mg| Sodium: 109.2mg.

142. EASY AIR FRYER APPLE PIES

Prep Time: 15 mins

Cook Time: 10 mins

Total Time: 25 mins

Ingredient

- 1 (14.1 ounces) package refrigerated pie crusts (2 pie crusts)
- 1 (21 ounces) can apple pie filling
- 1 egg, beaten
- 2 tablespoons cinnamon sugar, or to taste
- 1 serving cooking spray

Instructions

- Place 1 pie crust onto a lightly floured surface and roll out the dough with a rolling pin. Using a 2-1/4-inch round biscuit or cookie cutter cut the pie crust into 10 circles. Repeat with the second pie crust for a total of 20 pie crust circles.
- Fill about 1/2 of each circle with apple pie filling. Place a second pie crust circle on top, making a mini pie. Do not overfill. Press down the edges of the mini pies, crimping with a fork to seal. Brush tops with beaten egg and sprinkles with cinnamon sugar.
- Preheat the air fryer to 360 degrees F (175 degrees C).
- Lightly spray the air fryer basket with cooking spray. Place a batch of the mini pies in the air fryer basket, leaving space around each for air circulation.
- Bake until golden brown, 5 to 7 minutes. Remove from the basket and bake the remaining pies. Serve warm or at room temperature.

Nutrition Facts

- Calories: 264| Protein: 2.9g| Carbohydrates: 35g| Fat: 12.8g| Cholesterol: 16.4mg| Sodium: 225mg.

143. CHOCOLATE CAKE IN AN AIR FRYER

Prep Time: 10 mins

Cook Time: 15 mins

Total Time: 25 mins

Ingredient

- Cooking spray
- ¼ cup white sugar
- 3 ½ tablespoons butter, softened
- 1 egg
- 1 tablespoon apricot jam
- 6 tablespoons all-purpose flour

- 1 tablespoon unsweetened cocoa powder
- Salt to taste

Instructions

- Preheat an air fryer to 320 degrees F (160 degrees C). Spray a small fluted tube pan with cooking spray.
- Beat sugar and butter together in a bowl using an electric mixer until light and creamy. Add egg and jam; mix until combined. Sift in flour, cocoa powder, and salt; mix thoroughly. Pour batter into the prepared pan. Level the surface of the batter with the back of a spoon.
- Place pan in the air fryer basket. Cook until a toothpick inserted into the center of the cake comes out cleanly, about 15 minutes.

Nutrition Facts

- Calories: 214| Protein: 3.2g| Carbohydrates: 25.5g| Fat: 11.7g| Cholesterol: 73.2mg| Sodium: 130.3mg.

144. ZUCCHINI FRIES

Prep: 15 mins

Cook Time: 10 mins

Total Time: 25 mins

Ingredients

- 2 medium zucchini
- 1/2 cup flour
- 3 eggs
- Kosher salt and freshly ground black pepper
- 1/2 cup panko bread crumbs
- 1/2 cup Italian bread crumbs
- 1/4 cup parmesan cheese
- 1 Tablespoon extra virgin olive oil
- 1 teaspoon cumin
- Lemon Tarragon Aioli
- 1 egg
- 2 cloves garlic minced
- 3 teaspoons lemon juice plus 1 teaspoon lemon zest
- 1/2 cup canola oil
- 1/4 cup extra-virgin olive oil
- Kosher salt and freshly ground black pepper
- 2 Tablespoons minced fresh tarragon leaves

Instructions

Cut the zucchini into sticks no more than 1/2 inch thick and 3 inches long.

Add the flour to a shallow bowl. In a separate shallow bowl whisk the egg and season with salt and pepper. In a third shallow bowl, combine the panko, bread crumbs, parmesan cheese, olive oil and cumin.

Dredge zucchini in flour, then eggs, then Panko mixture.

Heat air fryer to 400 degrees.

Working in batches, place the zucchini fries in a single layer in the air fryer. Cook for 8-10 minutes, until crispy. Season with kosher salt while warm.

LEMON TARRAGON AIOLI:

While the fries cooking, prepare the aioli.

Combine egg, garlic, and lemon juice in a blender or food processor. With the motor running, slowly drizzle in the canola oil until emulsified.

Transfer to a medium bowl. Whisk the aioli while slowly drizzling in the olive oil. Fold in the tarragon leaves and lemon zest and season with salt and pepper, to taste

Nutrition

Calories: 433kcal | Carbohydrates: 21g | Protein: 9g | Fat: 35g | Saturated
Fat: 4g | Cholesterol: 112mg | Sodium: 285mg | Potassium: 261mg | Fiber: 1g | Sugar: 2g | Vitamin

A: 340IU | Vitamin C: 13.3mg | Calcium: 108mg | Iron: 2.3mg

145. AIR FRYER SHORTBREAD COOKIE FRIES

Prep Time: 20 mins

Cook Time: 10 mins

Total Time: 30 mins

Ingredient

- 1 ¼ cups all-purpose flour
- 3 tablespoons white sugar
- ½ cup butter
- ⅓ cup strawberry jam
- ⅛ teaspoon ground dried chipotle pepper (Optional)
- ⅓ cup lemon curd

Instructions

- Combine flour and sugar in a medium bowl. Cut in butter with a pastry blender until the mixture resembles fine crumbs and starts to cling. Form the mixture into a ball and knead until smooth.
- Preheat an air fryer to 350 degrees F (190 degrees C).
- Roll dough to 1/4-inch thickness on a lightly floured surface. Cut into 1/2-inch-wide "fries" about 3- to 4-inch long. Sprinkle with additional sugar.
- Arrange fries in a single layer in the air fryer basket. Cook until lightly browned, 3 to 4 minutes. Let cool in the basket until firm enough to transfer to a wire rack to cool completely. Repeat with the remaining dough.
- To make strawberry "ketchup," press jam through a fine-mesh sieve using the back of a spoon. Stir in ground chipotle. Whip the lemon curd to make it a dippable consistency for the "mustard."
- Serve sugar cookie fries with strawberry ketchup and lemon curd mustard.

Nutrition Facts

- Calories: 88| Protein: 0.7g| Carbohydrates: 12.4g| Fat: 4.1g| Cholesterol: 13mg| Sodium: 30.2mg.

146. EASY AIR FRYER FRENCH TOAST STICKS

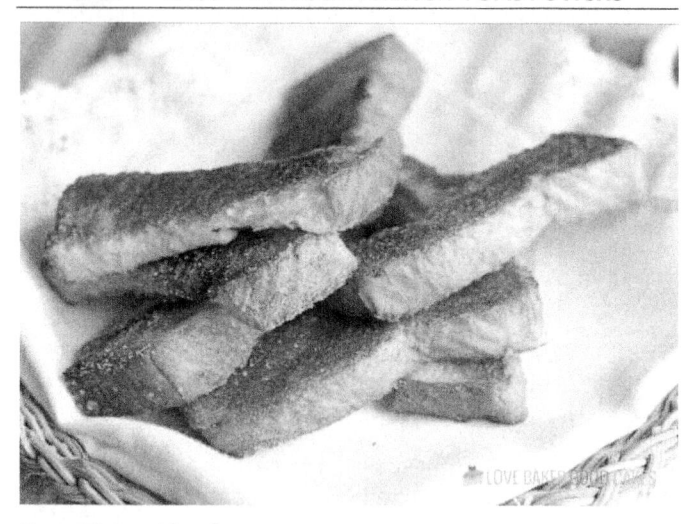

Prep Time: 10 mins

Cook Time: 10 mins

Total Time: 20 mins

Ingredient

- 4 slices of slightly stale thick bread, such as Texas toast
- parchment paper
- 2 eggs, lightly beaten
- ¼ cup milk
- 1 teaspoon vanilla extract
- 1 teaspoon cinnamon
- 1 pinch ground nutmeg (optional)

Instructions

- Cut each slice of bread into thirds to make sticks. Cut a piece of parchment paper to fit the bottom of the air fryer basket.
- Preheat air fryer to 360 degrees F (180 degrees C).
- Stir together eggs, milk, vanilla extract, cinnamon, and nutmeg in a bowl until well combined. Dip each piece of bread into the egg mixture, making sure each piece is well submerged. Shake each breadstick to remove excess liquid and place it in a single layer in the air fryer basket. Cook in batches, if necessary, to avoid overcrowding the fryer.
- Cook for 5 minutes, turn bread pieces and cook for an additional 5 minutes.

Nutrition Facts

- Calories: 232| Protein: 11.2g| Carbohydrates: 28.6g| Fat: 7.4g| Cholesterol: 188mg| Sodium: 423.4mg.

147. AIR FRYER PEANUT BUTTER & JELLY S'MORES

Prep Time: 5 mins

Cook Time: 5 mins

Total Time: 10 mins

Ingredient

- 1 chocolate-covered peanut butter cup
- 2 chocolate graham cracker squares, divided
- 1 teaspoon seedless raspberry jam
- 1 large marshmallow

Instructions

- Preheat the air fryer to 400 degrees F (200 degrees C).
- Place peanut butter cup on 1 graham cracker square. Top with jelly and marshmallow. Carefully place in an air fryer basket.
- Cook in preheated air fryer until marshmallow is lightly browned and softened, about 1 minute. Immediately top with the remaining graham cracker square.

Nutrition Facts

- Calories: 249| Protein: 3.9g| Carbohydrates: 41.8g| Fat: 8.2g| Cholesterol: 1mg| Sodium: 281.3mg.

148. AIR FRYER APPLE CIDER DONUT BITES

Prep Time: 10 mins

Cook Time: 10 mins

Additional Time: 30 mins

Total Time: 50 mins

Ingredient

- 2 ¼ cups all-purpose flour
- 3 tablespoons white sugar
- 4 teaspoons baking powder
- 1 ½ teaspoon apple pie spice
- ½ teaspoon salt
- 1 (4 ounces) container unsweetened applesauce
- ½ cup sparkling apple cider
- ¼ cup unsalted butter, melted and cooled
- 1 large egg
- 1 teaspoon apple cider vinegar

Glaze:

- 2 cups powdered sugar
- ½ teaspoon apple pie spice
- ¼ cup sparkling apple cider
- 1 teaspoon caramel extract (optional)

Instructions

- Preheat the air fryer to 400 degrees F (200 degrees C) for 5 minutes.
- Combine flour, sugar, baking powder, apple pie spice, and salt in a large bowl. Whisk together.
- Combine applesauce, sparkling apple cider, melted butter, egg, and vinegar in a small bowl; whisk until well combined. Add wet ingredients to the dry ingredients using a spatula and blend until just combined. Using a spring-hinged ice cream scoop, fill each cavity of the silicone donut mold with 2 tablespoons butter. Place the mold into the air fryer basket.
- Decrease temperature to 350 degrees F (175 degrees C) and cook for 8 minutes. Carefully turn out the donut bites and cook for an additional 2 minutes.
- Remove donut bites from the basket when done and let cool completely on a wire rack before glazing, about 30 minutes.
- Combine powdered sugar and apple pie spice in a small bowl and whisk together. Add sparkling apple cider and caramel extract; whisk together until the glaze is smooth.
- Dip each donut bite into the glaze, rolling it so that all sides are covered with the glaze. Set on a wire rack to allow the glaze to dry and harden

before eating.

Nutrition Facts

- Calories: 132| Protein: 1.7g| Carbohydrates: 25.9g| Fat: 2.6g| Cholesterol: 14.7mg| Sodium: 153.3mg.

149. CHOCOLATE SPONGE CAKE

Prep Time: 10 mins

Cook Time: 15 mins

Ingredients

- 3 large eggs
- 1 1/2 tbsp melted butter let cool until almost to room temperature
- 2 tbsp milk
- 2 tbsp sugar
- 1/4 tsp vanilla extract
- 1/3 cup cake flour
- 1/2 tsp baking powder
- 1 1/2 tbsp cocoa powder

Instructions

- Crack 3 eggs. Put the egg whites in a mixing bowl and egg yolks in a large bowl.
- To the egg yolks, add in the cooled butter, milk, sugar, and vanilla extract and mix until well combined. Sieve the cake flour, baking powder, and cocoa powder and whisk to combine the wet and dry ingredients to form a thick batter.
- In the meantime, use the electric mixer (or a whisk) to beat the egg whites until they can form a stiff peak. When done, pour this fluffy egg whites into the batter and gently combine them with a spatula until it is almost homogenous.
- Lightly grease the ramekins and put them inside the fryer basket. Preheat the air fryer at 400F (200C) for about 2 minutes.
- Scoop the batter into the preheated ramekins and air fry at 280F (140C) for about 10-12 minutes, until the toothpick comes out clean.

Nutrition

- Calories: 156kcal | Carbohydrates: 16g | Protein: 6g | Fat: 8g | Saturated Fat: 4g | Cholesterol: 135mg | Sodium: 89mg | Potassium: 145mg | Fiber: 1g | Sugar: 7g |

Vitamin A: 309IU | Calcium: 49mg | Iron: 1mg

150. RED BEAN WHEEL PIE

Prep Time: 10 mins

Cook Time: 10 mins

Ingredients

- 2 tbsp melted butter
- 2 eggs
- 2 tbsp sugar
- 1 tbsp honey
- 1/4 tsp vanilla extract
- 1/4 cup milk
- 1 cupcake flour
- 3/4 tsp baking powder
- 6 tbsp mashed sweetened red bean canned or homemade filling to taste

Instructions

- Lightly grease 4 ramekins with butter and place them in the fryer basket. Preheat at 400F (200C) for 2 minutes.
- In a large bowl, use a whisk to mix the egg, sugar, vanilla extract, and honey. Add in milk and whisk until the mixture is homogeneous. Finally, add in the sifted cake flour and baking powder. Continue to mix until everything is well blended.
- The total weight of the batter is about 280g. Spoon about 30g into the ramekin. Air fry at 300F (150C) for about 3 minutes.
- Take the desired amount of red bean (about 1 1/2 Tablespoon for mine) and roll it into a ball using the palms of your hand. Flatten it into a

circular disc that is smaller than the diameter of the ramekin. Place it in the center of the ramekin on top of the pancake. Scoop about 40g of the batter into the ramekins to cover the red beans.
- Air fry again at 300F (150C) for about 3 minutes. Brush some butter on top and air fry again at 300F (150C) for 1-2 minutes until the top is slightly golden brown.

Nutrition

- Calories: 284kcal | Carbohydrates: 47g | Protein: 8g | Fat: 9g | Saturated Fat: 5g | Cholesterol: 98mg | Sodium: 101mg | Potassium: 157mg | Fiber: 2g | Sugar: 20g | Calcium: 67mg | Iron: 1mg

151. SESAME CRUSTED SWEET POTATO CAKES

Prep Time: 15 mins

Cook Time: 10 mins

Ingredients

- 400 g mashed sweet potato
- 70 g tapioca starch
- 20 g cake flour
- sugar to taste
- 1/4 cup toasted sesame seeds

Instructions

- In a large mixing bowl, combine the mashed sweet potato, tapioca starch, cake flour, and sugar until homogenous.
- Roll the dough into a long strip. Cut the dough into one-inch pieces and roll them into a round ball. Flatten the balls with the palm of your hand to form patties.
- Sprinkle sesame seeds onto the patties and press the sesame seeds into the patties. Repeat this step for the other side.
- Spray oil to both sides and air fry at 380F (190C) for about 10 minutes, flip once in between.

Nutrition

- Calories: 108kcal | Carbohydrates: 21g | Protein: 2g | Fat: 2g | Saturated Fat: 1g | Sodium: 28mg | Potassium: 190mg | Fiber: 2g | Sugar: 2g | Vitamin C: 1mg | Calcium: 61mg | Iron: 1mg

152. STRAWBERRY PUFF PASTRY TWISTS

Prep Time: 10 mins

Cook Time: 10 mins

Ingredients

- 1 Puff pastry sheet defrosted and cut into two equal pieces
- 4-5 Tablespoon strawberry preserve

Instructions

- Spread the strawberry preserve on one piece of the puff pastry. Place the other piece on top. Using a sharp knife or a dough blade, cut the pastry dough "sandwich" into 1/2 inch wide strips.
- Twist each strip and place them in a parchment paper-lined fryer basket and air fry at 360F (180C) for 9-10 minutes, flip once in between.
- Let cool completely before serving.

Nutrition

- Calories: 393kcal | Carbohydrates: 41g | Protein: 5g | Fat: 23g | Saturated Fat: 6g | Sodium: 159mg | Potassium: 53mg | Fiber: 1g | Sugar: 10g | Vitamin C: 2mg | Calcium: 10mg | Iron: 2mg

153. MAPLE SPONGE CAKE

Prep Time: 10 mins

Cook Time: 15 mins

Ingredients

- 50 g cake flour
- 1/2 teaspoon baking powder
- 35 g melted butter and let it cool to almost room temperature
- 2 tablespoon milk
- 2 1/2 tablespoon maple syrup
- 1/4 teaspoon vanilla extract
- 3 large eggs

Instructions

- Crack 3 eggs and put the egg whites in the mixing bowl and egg yolks in a medium-sized bowl.
- To the egg yolks, add in the cooled butter, maple syrup, and vanilla extract and mix until well combined.
- In a separate large bowl, sieve the cake flour and baking powder and mix them. Pour the egg yolk mixture into this large bowl and gently whisk to combine the wet and dry ingredients to form a thick batter.
- In the meantime, use the electric mixer (or a whisk) to beat the egg whites until they can form a stiff peak. When done, pour this fluffy egg whites into the batter and gently combine them with a spatula until it is almost homogenous.
- Put the muffin tins inside the fryer basket, hold them down with a steamer rack and preheat the air fryer at 400F (200C) for about 2 minutes.
- Pour the batter into the preheated muffin tins and air fry at 260F (130C) for about 13 minutes until the toothpick comes out clean. Air fry at 380F (190C) again for about 1-2 minutes until the color turns golden brown.

Nutrition

- Calories: 195kcal | Carbohydrates: 18g | Protein: 6g | Fat: 11g | Saturated Fat: 6g | Cholesterol: 142mg | Sodium: 114mg | Potassium: 147mg | Fiber: 1g | Sugar: 8g | Calcium: 62mg | Iron: 1mg

154. ALMOND FLOUR CHOCOLATE BANANA NUT BROWNIE

Prep Time: 5 mins

Cook Time: 8 mins

Ingredients For Brownie:

- 1 large ripe banana
- 3 Tablespoons coconut oil melted
- 1 teaspoon vanilla extract
- 1 1/2 cups almond flour
- 1/3 cup chocolate whey protein powder
- 1/2 teaspoon baking soda
- 1/4 teaspoon salt

Other Ingredients:

- 1/4 cup chocolate chips or to taste
- 1/4 cup chopped walnuts or to taste

Instructions

- In a mixing bowl, mix all the ingredients, except chocolate chips and walnuts, until well combined. Fold in the chocolate chips and walnuts if desired.
- Line parchment paper in a 7-inch springform pan. Pour the batter into the pan and air fry at 300F (150C) for about 8 minutes.
- Let cool on a cooling rack. When cooled, cut it into 1-inch squares to serve.

Nutrition

- Calories:307kcal | Carbohydrates: 16g | Protein: 7g | Fat: 26g | Saturated Fat: 8g | Cholesterol: 1mg | Sodium: 194mg | Potassium: 92mg | Fiber: 4g | Sugar: 8g | Vitamin C: 2mg |

Calcium: 72mg | Iron: 1mg

Air fryer Healthy Recipes

155. AIR FRYER GREEN BEANS

Prep Time: 5 mins

Cook Time: 10 mins

Total Time: 15 mins

Ingredients

- 1 lb green beans
- 1 tbsp olive oil
- 1/2 tsp salt
- 1/4 tsp pepper

Instructions

- Trim the green beans, then toss with olive oil, salt, and pepper.
- Put prepared green beans in the air fryer basket and cook at 400F for 10 minutes, shaking the basket halfway through.

Nutrition

- Calories: 66kcal | Carbohydrates: 8g | Protein: 2g | Fat: 4g | Saturated Fat: 1g | Sodium: 298mg | Potassium: 239mg | Fiber: 3g | Sugar: 4g | Vitamin A: 782IU | Vitamin C: 14mg | Calcium: 42mg | Iron: 1mg

156. HEALTHY AIR FRYER CHICKEN AND VEGGIES (20 MINUTES!)

Prep Time: 5 minutes

Cook Time: 15 minutes

Total Time: 20 minutes

Ingredients

- 1 pound chicken breast, chopped into bite-size pieces (2-3 medium chicken breasts)
- 1 cup broccoli florets (fresh or frozen)
- 1 zucchini chopped
- 1 cup bell pepper chopped (any colors you like)
- 1/2 onion chopped
- 2 cloves garlic minced or crushed
- 2 tablespoons olive oil
- 1/2 teaspoon EACH garlic powder, chili powder, salt, pepper
- 1 tablespoon Italian seasoning (or spice blend of choice)

Instructions

- Preheat air fryer to 400F.
- Chop the veggies and chicken into small bite-size pieces and transfer to a large mixing bowl.
- Add the oil and seasoning to the bowl and toss to combine.
- Add the chicken and veggies to the preheated air fryer and cook for 10 minutes, shaking halfway, or until the chicken and veggies are charred and chicken is cooked through. If your air fryer is small, you may have to cook them in 2-3 batches.

Nutrition

- Serving: 1serving | Calories: 230kcal | Carbohydrates: 8g | Protein: 26g | Fat: 10g | Saturated Fat: 2g | Cholesterol: 73mg | Sodium: 437mg | Potassium: 734mg | Fiber: 3g | Sugar: 4g | Vitamin A: 1584IU | Vitamin C: 79mg | Calcium: 50mg | Iron: 1mg

157. FRIED GREEN BEANS (AIR FRYER)

Prep Time: 5 minutes

Cook Time: 5 minutes

Total Time: 10 minutes

Ingredients

- 1 lb. fresh green beans (cleaned and trimmed)
- 1 tsp. oil
- 1/4 tsp. garlic powder
- 1/8 tsp. sea salt

Instructions

- Toss all the ingredients together in a bowl to coat the green beans with oil and spices.
- Transfer about half of the green beans to the air fryer basket. (You'll have to do this in two batches or the beans won't cook properly) Spread them out as evenly as possible and return the basket to the air fryer.
- Adjust temp to 400 and set time to 5 minutes, or whichever time you chose from the chart above, and press start.
- When done, remove the basket from the fryer and turn the beans out onto a platter (repeat with the second half of the beans).
- If you try the beans and they aren't cooked enough to your liking, simply return them to the air fryer in the basket and cook in 2-minute increments until they are cooked to your liking.
- Cool slightly and serve.

Nutrition

- Serving: 0.25the recipe | Calories: 47kcal | Carbohydrates: 8g | Protein: 2g | Fat: 1g | Saturated Fat: 1g | Sodium: 67mg | Potassium: 239mg | Fiber: 3g | Sugar: 4g | Vitamin A: 782IU | Vitamin C: 14mg | Calcium: 42mg | Iron: 1mg

158. AIR FRYER GREEN BEANS WITH BACON

Print Recipe Rate Recipe

Prep Time: 15 minutes

Cook Time: 10 minutes

Total Time: 25 minutes

Ingredients

- 3 cups (330 g) Frozen Cut Green Beans
- 3 slices (3 slices) bacon, diced
- 1/4 cup (62.5 ml) Water
- 1 teaspoon (1 teaspoon) Kosher Salt
- 1 teaspoon (1 teaspoon) Ground Black Pepper

Instructions

- Place the frozen green beans, onion, bacon, and water in a 6 x 3-inch heatproof pan.
- Place the pan in the air fryer basket. Set air fryer to 375°F for 15 minutes.
- Raise the air fryer temperature to 400°F for 5 minutes. Add salt and pepper to taste and toss well.
- Remove from the air fryer and cover the pan. Let it rest for 5 minutes and serve.
- I find that frozen vegetables often cook up better in an air fryer if you're looking for moist, tender beans.

- If you want crispy beans, you should start with fresh beans rather than frozen.
- You can also substitute cooked sausage for the bacon.
- If you use lean chicken sausage, then you may have to spray the beans with a little oil to get the best "air-fried" texture from them.

Nutrition

- Calories: 95kcal | Carbohydrates: 6g | Protein: 3g | Fat: 6g | Fiber: 2g | Sugar: 2g

159. AIR FRYER STUFFED PEPPERS

Prep Time: 15 Minutes

Cook Time: 15 Minutes

Total Time: 30 Minutes

Ingredients

- 6 Green Bell Peppers
- 1 Lb Lean Ground Beef
- 1 Tbsp Olive Oil
- 1/4 Cup Green Onion Diced
- 1/4 Cup Fresh Parsley
- 1/2 Tsp Ground Sage
- 1/2 Tsp Garlic Salt
- 1 Cup Cooked Rice
- 1 Cup Marinara Sauce More to Taste
- 1/4 Cup Shredded Mozzarella Cheese

Instructions

- Warm-up a medium-sized skillet with the ground beef and cook until well done.
- Drain the beef and return to the pan.
- Add in the olive oil, green onion, parsley, sage, and salt. Mix this well.
- Add in the cooked rice and marinara, mix well.
- Cut the top off of each pepper and clean the seeds out.
- Scoop the mixture into each of the peppers and place it in the basket of the air fryer. (I did 4 the first round, 2 the second to make them fit.)
- Cook for 10 minutes at 355*, carefully open and add cheese.
- Cook for an additional 5 minutes or until peppers are slightly soft and cheese is melted.
- Serve.

Nutrition Information

- Calories: 296| Total Fat: 13g| Saturated Fat: 4g| Trans Fat: 0g| Unsaturated Fat: 7g| Cholesterol: 70mg| Sodium: 419mg| Carbohydrates: 19g| Fiber: 2g| Sugar: 6g| Protein: 25g

- **4 WEEKS MEAL PLAN**

WEEK 1

	BREAKFAST	LUNCH	DINNER
MONDAY	Sausage Breakfast Casserole	Sexy Air-Fried Meatloaf	Steak Bites With Mushrooms
TUESDAY	Tasty Baked Eggs	Air Fryer Crab Rangoon	Ranch Pork Chops
WEDNESDAY	Blueberry Muffin	Italian Sausage Patties	Lemon-Garlic Air Fryer Salmon
THURSDAY	Air Fryer Breakfast Frittata	Ham and Mozzarella Eggplant Boats	Chimichangas
FRIDAY	Airfryer French Toast Sticks	Air Fryer Cauliflower Fried Rice	Leftover Turkey and Mushroom Sandwich
SATURDAY	Parmesan Truffle Oil Fries	Leftover Turkey and Mushroom Sandwich	Sesame-Crusted Cod With Snap Peas
SUNDAY	Bang Bang Fried Shrimp	Popcorn Chicken Gizzards	Ham and Mozzarella Eggplant Boats

WEEK 2

	BREAKFAST	LUNCH	DINNER
MONDAY	Sausage Breakfast Casserole	Rib-Eye Steak	Halibut Sitka
TUESDAY	Airfryer French Toast Sticks	Meatloaf	Italian-Style Meatballs
WEDNESDAY	Baked Eggs Cup	Air Fryer Steak And Cheese Melts	Shrimp and Mushroom Risotto
THURSDAY	Easy Cherry Turnovers	Italian Sausage Patties	Chimichangas
FRIDAY	Tasty Baked Eggs	Air Fryer Salmon For One	Taco Calzones
SATURDAY	Breakfast Potatoes In the Air Fryer	Ham and Mozzarella Eggplant Boats	Mexican-Style Air Fryer Stuffed Chicken Breasts
SUNDAY	Blueberry Muffin	Sexy Air-Fried Meatloaf	Leftover Turkey and Mushroom Sandwich

WEEK 3

	BREAKFAST	LUNCH	DINNER
MONDAY	Breakfast Potatoes In the Air Fryer	Rib-Eye Steak	Steak Fajitas
TUESDAY	Air Fryer Breakfast Frittata	Fish Sticks	Stuffed Peppers
WEDNESDAY	Tasty Baked Eggs	Easy Air Fryer French Toast Sticks	Garlic Parmesan Air Fried Shrimp Recipe
THURSDAY	Loaded Hash Brown	Meatloaf	Cheesy Bacon Wrapped Shrimp
FRIDAY	Blueberry Muffin	Air-Fried Popcorn Chicken Gizzards	Coconut Shrimp
SATURDAY	Easy Cherry Turnovers	Air Fryer Cauliflower Fried Rice	Pecan Crusted Salmon
SUNDAY	Bang Bang Fried Shrimp	Air Fryer Steak And Cheese Melts	Sesame-Crusted Cod With Snap Peas

WEEK 4

	BREAKFAST	LUNCH	DINNER
MONDAY	Parmesan Truffle Oil Fries	Crab Rangoon	Roasted Brussels Sprouts
TUESDAY	Sausage Breakfast Casserole	Wiener Schnitzel	Wasabi Lime Steak
WEDNESDAY	Airfryer French Toast Sticks	Popcorn Chicken Gizzards	Five Spices Salt And Pepper Pork
THURSDAY	Breakfast Potatoes In the Air Fryer	Easy Air Fryer French Toast Sticks	Seared Scallops With Jalapeno Vinaigrette
FRIDAY	Baked Eggs Cup	Air Fryer Salmon For One	Roasted Veggies
SATURDAY	Tasty Baked Eggs	Air Fryer Crab Rangoon	Korean Marinated Pork Belly
SUNDAY	Loaded Hash Brown	Air-Fried Popcorn Chicken Gizzards	Taco Calzones

Printed in Great Britain
by Amazon